To my Savior
I was lost and could not find You
You embraced me and said
I will not forget you
See, I have engraved you on the palms of My hands

ISAIAH 49: 15B, 16A

Contents

Acknowledgments

To my Lord and Savior, I extend my deepest gratitude. Thank You for Your dying love. Through my pain I have come to know You in ways I never thought were possible. I have been broken, but not forsaken—to God be the glory!

To my mom, Shirley Henderson, you encouraged and prayed for me every day to finish my manuscript. Ever since I was a little girl, you have taught me about Jesus. Thank you for being a living example of His love and faithfulness. I love you, Mom!

To my uncle, Harold Buckley (Uncle Tiny), you have always been a tremendous father figure, uncle, and friend to me. I will forever cherish your hugs, kisses and our special times together. You are my hero! To my aunts Elaine and Nina, and my brother David, thank you for your encouragement. To my nieces Kami and Chanel, I see Jesus' love through your smiles and laughter. I love you all dearly!

To my dearest friend, Sherry Frattini, I had always longed to have a sister. Twenty years ago God graciously allowed our paths to meet. Thank you my sister, my friend.

To my treasured friends and family, thank you for your love, support, thoughtfulness, and prayers. I regret that I cannot name each of you individually, but you know who you are and I love you!

Special thanks to my publisher, Steve Laube, and ACW Press, for making this book possible.

IN LOVING MEMORY—To Ken, my gallant knight, this is your story. Your work for Christ continues. To Daddy, my Hercules; to Grandma Buckley, my role model; to Uncle Kenneth, my adviser; to Uncle Rolland, Aunt Marjorie, and Grandpa and Grandma Henderson—I miss you, I love you, and I cannot wait for heaven's reunion!

SHERRY M. JONES

CHAPTER ONE

The Accident

The Lord is my light and my salvation:
whom shall I fear?
The Lord is the strength of my life;
of whom shall I be afraid?
Though an host should encamp against me,
my heart shall not fear;
though war should rise against
me, in this will I be confident.
PSALM 27: 1, 3, KJV

*K*en squeezed my hand in the dark. The sun was falling behind the dried-out January cornfields as our van approached a farmhouse sheltered by a dense line of trees. Directly beyond the house I noticed a railroad crossing sign.

Suddenly, a powerful locomotive blasted from behind the thick windbreak of trees. It swiftly raced toward our van. Terrified screams ricocheted off the frosted windows. "STOP! A TRAIN!"

In a split-second decision, the driver gunned the accelerator. The spinning tires burned rubber skidmarks across the wet pavement. Just as our vehicle crossed the tracks the freight train was only inches away. Within seconds the monstrous beast slammed into the right side of our van and traveled forward two hundred yards before it came to a screeching halt. The van spun wildly into a complete three-sixty turn, spraying sheet metal and broken glass all around.

My husband Ken and I, and his uncle, were hurled sixty feet from the van into the blistering Iowa winds. Jutting rocks on the ground pierced our flesh like stakes as centrifugal force plunged our bodies face down. We landed within ten feet of each other in a frozen, snow-packed ditch. The entire right side of the vehicle was missing; sharp metal fragments outlined the frame where the doors and windows had been. The other three passengers remained in the van, with only minor injuries.

Distant voices echoed. "Hey, lady, are you okay?"

My mind was enveloped in darkness as I lay on the frozen ground. I struggled to stay awake. My thoughts drifted. *What happened? I died!* A sudden peacefulness replaced the fear and confusion. I felt my spirit drift away as my last breath vaporized into eternity.

Within minutes, a God-given breath miraculously resuscitated my heart.

A deep voice shouted, "She's unresponsive! I can't get a pulse!"

A disheartened plea became clearer. "Miss, can you hear me?"

Help me! I screamed from within.

Then a harsh demand, "Are you okay? Talk to us!"

My mind was spinning. *I hurt so badly! I need to answer them.* Painfully I whispered, "I'm here."

A deep voice rumbled, "She's alive! She's alive!"

My arms and legs were numb. I strained my eyes to focus on the men lifting me from the ground. Through the muffled sound of whirling propellers I silently cried, *Jesus! Jesus! Oh my God, help me!*

Disoriented in the blackness, I heard, "We're cutting off your coat. Stay with us. Are you still with us?"

I moaned softly. *They're cutting off my clothes? Oh, God, what's going on?*

Another voice instructed, "Okay, now we're cutting off your pretty sweater. Stay with us. What's your name?"

"Sherry."

"What's your last name?" a man asked.

"Jones. Sherry Jones."

"Where are you?"

"Somewhere in Iowa…I think."

Another demand followed. "Stay with us. Don't close your eyes. Talk to us!"

"Hmm? I'm cold. It's so cold!" I sobbed.

A deep voice commanded, "Sherry, you need to stay alert!"

Ken, help me! I pleaded.

Once securely fastened inside the helicopter, I was whisked away. The relentless questions continued throughout the remainder of the flight. "Who are you? Where are you?"

I was so annoyed. The pain was excruciating. *Don't they know who I am by now? Why do they keep asking me who and where I am? I want to close my eyes. I want this nightmare to end.*

"Are you allergic to any medications?" someone asked.

"No. Where's Ken?"

"Ma'am, we don't know. The others were taken to a different hospital," came the reply.

"I want Ken!" I cried.

"Are you on any medications?"

"Synthroid," I replied.

"Thyroid meds?"

"Yes." I answered. *What hospital? Where did they take Ken?*

"Do you have any diseases?"

"Yes, cancer!" I cried in despair.

Engulfed in pain and confusion, I struggled to survive.

CHAPTER TWO

Helicopter to Heaven

*For the Lord your God is God of gods
and Lord of lords, the great God,
mighty and awesome, who shows no partiality...
He defends the cause of the fatherless and the widow.*
DEUTERONOMY 10: 17A & 18A

*I*t was a warm cloudy summer afternoon. I was seven years old and liked the breeze caressing my face as I rode my blue and silver bicycle. I could not wander far from home, so I rode up and down our street admiring all the bright delicate flowers in the neighbors' gardens. Suddenly the billowy clouds became dark. The lofty, gray skies merged into a mighty force, and big drops of rain started to fall from the sky. The raindrops quickly turned into powerful pellets, like little white frozen peas. The brutal hail pounded harshly on my tender head. I could not get my bike to stop wobbling, and it toppled over. My screams echoed off the pavement as I lay next to my bike. Within moments Daddy dashed out the front door of the beautiful tri-level brick house that he and my grandpa had built for us, brick

Seven years old

by brick, with their strong hands. He reached down, put his warm and loving arms around me, and picked me up. His arms sheltered me from the violent raging storm, and once inside, Daddy lovingly embraced "his girl." He was my Hercules.

I thought my daddy was the strongest and most handsome man in the neighborhood. He towered above me, could move most of our furniture by himself, and maintained a perpetual sun-bronzed ruddy complexion. Daddy and my grandpa owned a masonry construction company, and spent countless hours of strenuous labor under the heat and bright light of the sun.

Grandpa and Daddy pause for a photo break with David and me while building our new brick home.

Sunday was probably my favorite day of the week, because I knew that Daddy would be with me the entire day, and I loved going to church. My parents called me their little missionary. After church Mama, Daddy, my brother David, and I would have lunch together at either Furr's Cafeteria or The Drumstick Restaurant, or we would drive home and eat Mama's prize-winning meat loaf. The tantalizing aroma of freshly baked blueberry muffins permeated the kitchen. After a satisfying meal, we would climb into our family's big blue station wagon for a Sunday drive. One of our favorite outings was to the airport to watch the planes land. When we got out of the car, David and I would race to see who could get to the fence first. Our fingers intertwined in the cool metal openings of the chain links. We would lean our heads backward, squinting toward the sky while the sun's reflection mirrored off the huge silver planes that circled above us. The noise was so loud we would cup our hands over our ears to stifle the sound. After the planes glided miles down the long runways, we would lose sight of them. Then we would play games or have more races until the next plane circled overhead.

Mama was the leader of my Blue Bird troop.
I'm to the left of Mama.

We were a close-knit family. My maternal grandmother, Grandma Buckley, would come to our house nearly every day. She was petite, just slightly under five feet, but stood tall in my eyes. She had unshakable faith in God and was a great storyteller. Sometimes she would even play dolls with me.

My childhood Christmases are some of my fondest memories. My family of four, my grandma, and my mom's extended family would go over to my Uncle Kenneth's and Aunt Nina's house every year for Christmas dinner and gift exchanges. Aunt Nina is a wonderful cook and made the most succulent dinners, with turkey, dressing, and all the trimmings. My uncles called me "Dolly" and were very attentive. Of course, I was always Daddy's girl.

My perception of heavenly Father was parallel to my image of my earthly father. I knew that they loved me, enjoyed spending time with me, and would shelter me from the storms of life.

Aunt Nina and
Uncle Kenneth
with Christmas dinner

Grandma Buckley, Mama and me with
my favorite doll Chatty Cathy

Our first formal family portrait
when I was seven years old

On a cool February afternoon in 1977, I was a first-year student in high school. I arrived home to find my mom and dad in the office. Mom was ironing, and Dad was estimating a job from a large set of blueprints. Seven months earlier, Dad had suffered a severe heart attack and sold his masonry company to become an estimator. I liked coming home and knowing that both parents would be there. Since Dad was working out of our home, we spent more quality time together. He was a great math whiz and helped me analyze the most difficult algebra problems.

I made myself a sandwich and decided to tune in for an episode of "The Brady Bunch," a hit television sitcom of that decade. David went to Burger King to get a late lunch.

Startled by the sudden pounding of footsteps racing down the stairs, I turned to look in their direction. Mom's eyes were filled with fright. "Sherry, I think Dad is having another heart attack!" she shouted.

"A heart attack? Oh, God! No!" I cried.

With her hands trembling at her sides, Mom pleaded, "You probably know what to do."

Mom knew that I had recently completed a basic first aid class. Really, though, I knew nothing about how to administer CPR. My bologna sandwich flew into the air as I jumped to my feet.

My heart raced as I ran into the office. *God, what should I do? Help me!* I prayed. Dad was reclined in his chair with his back facing the door, so I cautiously stepped in front of him. His blue eyes were rolled back into his head so only the whites showed. His face was purple, and he was gasping for air. "Dad-deeee!" I shrilled.

Words did not come out of his mouth. His asphyxiated breaths were ragged and painful.

"Dad, I'm here! Can you hear me? Please, Dad!" I begged.

He remained unresponsive. *What do we do? God help us!* I pleaded.

Mom stayed by my dad's side as I sprinted upstairs to my bedroom to get my first aid book. Hurriedly flipping through the chapters, I looked for anything that resembled heart attacks. The only information it contained for a heart attack victim was to make sure the person was lying down and comfortable. I flung the book across the room and ran down the stairs to the office. Meanwhile, Mom had called the doctor.

Catching my breath, I said, "The book says to lay him flat on his back."

Mom and I managed to lower his heavy body to the floor. His breathing continued to be labored, as he struggled and gasped for air. I pleaded, "Jesus, help my daddy! Don't let him die!"

Dad continued wheezing, coughing, and choking uncontrollably. I felt like a foreigner, clueless about how to handle any type of life and death situation. As he fought for his last breath, I wiped the fluid from his mouth and administered mouth-to-mouth resuscitation.

Nothing changed.

I tried to resuscitate him again. "Lord Jesus, help! I don't know what to do! Dad, I love you! Please, don't die!" I sobbed as I tightly clenched his hand.

Moments later distant sirens roared closer. A loud knock pounded on the front door, and four uniformed men filed through the hallways carrying heavy black bags and equipment. "Cardiac arrest!" a voice exclaimed.

I watched helplessly as they cut off Dad's shirt. "Clear!" yelled the man who held the defibrillator.

Dad's chest popped up from the ground. The men hustled around the room shouting orders and exchanging supplies. Then someone said, "We're not getting a pulse!"

Dad, breathe! Please, Daddy! I whispered.

The paramedics carried my dad out the front door on a gurney. They told Mom they would continue to try to revive him in the helicopter that had landed in front of our house. Dozens of curious onlookers swarmed to the neighbor's front yard. I decided that the view from my bedroom would be more private, so I sprinted up the stairs and looked out the window. Within seconds the sound of the helicopter's propellers faded away behind the neighbor's house that blocked the view. I cried out, "Good-bye, Daddy."

I had an overwhelming sensation that he was not coming back. On the way to the hospital, I clutched my small red Bible and silently quoted Psalm 23 from memory. *The Lord is my Shepherd; I shall not want.... Yea, though I walk through the valley of the shadow of death, I will fear no evil: for Thou art with me; Thy rod and Thy staff they comfort me* (KJV).

We arrived at the hospital's emergency room and approached the nurse's station. "We're here to see Roy Henderson," Mom said.

"Are you family?" the nurse asked.

"Yes, I'm his wife, and this is our daughter," Mom replied.

"Wait one moment, please," the nurse said as she walked from the counter. She returned with a solemn look on her face. "Please be seated. The doctor will be here shortly. She needs to speak with you."

"I want to see my husband. What's going on?" Mom pleaded.

"The doctor will be right with you!" the nurse replied brusquely.

Minutes felt like hours as I paced back and forth in front of the nurses' station. "Mom, what's taking so long?" I begged.

"Honey, I don't know!" she replied wearily.

Time continued to drag until a middle-aged, dark-haired lady wearing a long white coat and silver-rimmed glasses came walking toward Mom and me. "Mrs. Henderson?" she asked.

"Yes?" Mom replied.

"May I speak with you in private?" she said, as she pointed toward the window.

Our last family portrait.
Three months before Daddy died.

"Sherry, I'll be right back. You wait here,"Mom instructed.

Tired of pacing the lobby, I looked for a drinking fountain. Leaning forward, I felt the wet drops arc up and soothe my parched lips. I quickly turned around when suffocated sobs echoed across the lobby. As the doctor removed her embrace from Mom's shoulders, Mom turned away from her and hurriedly walked toward me with tear-filled eyes.

"Oh, Honey!" Mom exclaimed as she hugged me close. "The doctor said that Daddy died!"

"Daddy is dead?" I cried out in disbelief. "Mom, what are we going to do?"

"Honey, I don't know. Somehow we'll make it. God will help us. I know He will," she managed to say.

Mom's faith in God was her sustaining power. Her high school sweetheart, who was her husband of twenty-one years, was gone. Dad's death left an incredible void in all our lives. I returned to school a week later and noticed that all the students were loading onto the buses for a field trip. I did not feel like laughing and having fun. I felt numb. I stared out the window for most of the bus ride and wondered if the emptiness I felt would last forever.

The following summer I was thrilled when I made the cheerleading squad, but missed my dad's approval. I had a peaceful feeling, though, that since it was such a special occasion, that God may have propped open a little window from heaven. I could hear my dad cheering from heaven's grandstands as he shouted, "That's my girl!"

God soon filled my emptiness with extracurricular activities. When the school year started I was elected class president, sang in the school choir, and was on the newspaper and yearbook staffs. A few months later I got my driver's license and my first official job, selling sunglasses in a booth at the mall. I also started to date a kind Christian boy who was a basketball player. Dad had loved basketball. I knew he would have liked my new boyfriend, too.

Dad's death had a lasting impact on my life, and also, I believe, changed my perception of God, due to the paral-

Grandma Buckley and me.

lels that I saw between them. Since my father had left me, although it was not by choice, I felt that God would forsake me too, leaving me to face life's challenges alone.

Only three short years after Dad's death, Grandma Buckley also died of heart failure. Her life span had doubled that of my father as she was eighty-two years old. We had become best friends and my heart longed for her too. Two weeks before her death God had given me a dream about her. In that dream, I entered her kitchen and found her lying on the floor next to her bird cage. I kneeled down beside her and cried, "Grandma? Grandma, are you okay?" She responded in an almost angelic voice, "It's okay, I'm going to be all right."

I knew that Grandma was with Jesus too, but I missed our special times and hearing her wonderful stories.

CHAPTER THREE

Gallant Knight

Though one may be overpowered,
two can defend themselves.
A cord of three strands
is not quickly broken.
ECCLESIASTES 4: 12

When I graduated from high school, I started to pray that God would prepare me to meet my future husband. The predominant dream I had was to get married, have children, and live happily ever after. After I graduated from the University of Colorado, I entered corporate America. I worked mid-management marketing positions, received promotions, and felt fulfilled by my career. I even did some modeling.

The one thing missing in my life was having a family of my own. Through the many years of loneliness, broken-heartedness, and unfulfilled dreams that followed, I often questioned God's plan for my life. When I celebrated my thirtieth birthday, I cringed to think that I might be single all my life.

Then, one day—I met my prince!

A couple of months after my thirty-first birthday, I attended a church dance and met a wonderful man who was also an excellent dancer. At one point as we were twirling around the dance floor, I looked into his baby blue eyes and thought, *He is so handsome.*

On our first date Ken brought me a beautiful bouquet of wild flowers. We continued to date, and each time we were together I learned more about what an incredible man Ken was in so many ways. As our relationship grew deeper, we often read the Bible together. I was so thankful that God had brought this wonderful, godly man into my life.

People have often asked me when I realized that Ken was the man for me. I knew quite early in our relationship, probably even by our third date. The more I learned of Ken, his relationship with our Lord, his goals, his desires, and his love for life, the more I realized that a man with his sincerity and character was the one for whom I had waited all my life. After dating a few months, we listed our prayer requests. Ken coyly requested, "When I ask Sherry to marry me that she will say, 'Yes!'"

Inside, I was saying, *I will! I will!* Yet outside, I smiled sweetly and held his hand.

After Ken hinted of his pending marriage proposal, each time we were together I wondered if this would be the day that Ken would ask me to marry him. That moment came on a beautiful summer day in June. Ken planned a picnic to his favorite getaway in the Rockies. As we started our drive on the winding road, we approached a scenic overlook where Ken suggested we pull over to take some pictures.

"Sure, sounds like fun," I answered.

As Ken prepared the timer on his camera and adjusted it on the tripod to take some pictures of us, I gazed out at the majestic mountains. We sat on a stone wall with the picturesque panorama as our backdrop. I was ecstatic and could hardly contain my enthusiasm when this wonderful man looked into my eyes and asked those four beautiful words, "Will you marry me?"

Engaged! Showing off my sparkling new engagement ring.

Inside I was screaming, *YES, YES, YES! A thousand times, YES!* I looked at Ken and then down at the sparkling diamond that he held in his hand. As I looked at Ken again, the camera flashed and clicked. With more conviction than at any other time in my life, I replied, "Yes, I will be honored to marry you!"

Ken gently slid the ring on my finger. It was the greatest moment of my life.

My prayers had truly been answered: *Now to him who is able to do immeasurably more than all we ask or imagine, according to his power and work within us, to him be glory in the church and in Christ Jesus throughout all generations, for ever and ever! Amen.* (Ephesians 3: 20 & 21).

Ken and me on our engagement day.

꙼꙼

It was a gorgeous fall day in early October. The gold and red hues of the aspens were highlighted by a bright sun ray that burst through the drifting clouds. Cascading snow glistened from the mountain peaks of Colorado, creating a warm ambience for the beautiful drive to our wedding chapel. Ken and I had found a quaint country chapel that was nestled in the majestic Rockies and surrounded by large evergreen trees. In front of the church was a historic bell, which was rung after we said our vows.

When I stepped out of the car, I was greeted by nature's symphony of wild birds singing from the branches of the evergreens. Crickets nestled in the scattered pinecones echoed harmonious melodies. The morning air was brisk and invigorating, and the scent of pine filled the air.

With my wedding gown draped over my arm, I entered the bride's room and stretched my arm up high to place the hanger over the top of the door. When I turned around, my mom was quietly standing in the doorway. Proudly, with tears in her eyes, she said, "My precious daughter is getting married!"

"Oh, Mom, can you believe it? God is so good to bless me with Ken!" I said.

"Yes, He is good! This is your special day! I'm so happy for you and Ken. Here, Dear, let me help you with your dress. Just look at this intricate beadwork! See how the sequins shimmer in the sunlight!" Mom exclaimed, as she brought the gown near the window.

"I'm thrilled that I did some modeling for the bridal boutique. When I tried on all the dresses for the shows, I just knew this was the perfect one for me!" I exclaimed.

I carefully stepped into my beaded gown and slid each arm into its delicate sleeve. Mom gently slid the zipper up my back. When I turned around, she lovingly said, "You're the most beautiful bride in the world! We have prayed for so long that this day would come. Always remember to have Christ at the center of your marriage, like Daddy and I did in ours, and you'll never be sorry."

"We will, Mom," I said, as I paused to reach for a tissue. "You have always loved and encouraged me. You're the best mom in the world! I love you so much."

A couple of my bridesmaids entered the room. "Isn't this exciting? I'm finally the bride! I'm going to meet with Ken now."

"Oh, no, you can't do that! The groom can't see the bride before the wedding. It's tradition!" the coordinator replied.

"It's really important to Ken and me to pray together before the ceremony. We want to feel God's presence before we say our vows," I said.

When I entered the prayer room, Ken exclaimed, "Wow! What a bo-da-cious babe!"

"Why, thank you very much!" I said proudly, as I twirled around. "You are so handsome, too, my love!"

"Can you believe that in less than one hour, we'll be married?" Ken marveled.

"This is the happiest day of my life! I love you so much!" I joyfully exclaimed.

"I love you too, B.B.!" Ken replied.

Ken reached for my hand as we walked over to the sofa. "Let's pray," Ken said, as he bowed his head. "Dear God, thank You for my beautiful bride. I can't believe she's mine. You answered my prayers in a huge way. Please help me to be a loving husband. We love You and invite You to be the head of our marriage and all that we do. Bless us today, Lord."

I prayed, "Dear Heavenly Father, thank You so much for blessing me. Ken is so sweet, kind, and sensitive. Father, we want to glorify You in all that we do today. Please anoint the words of the pastor. If anybody here doesn't know You today, we pray that You will minister to them through our songs, vows, and prayers. In Your name we ask. Amen." I gave Ken's hand a slight squeeze and opened my eyes.

When I walked back to the bride's room, my feet felt weightless, as if I were gliding through large puffy clouds. I had never thought that my life could be so incredibly happy. All of the planning and preparations had now become a reality. I stood in the atrium and looked through the small one-way glass to the chapel. My attendants were beautifully adorned in purple moiré taffeta off-the-shoulder gowns, and stood aligned at the front of the sanctuary. Each of them had such a special place in my heart.

Uncle Harold and I stayed concealed outside the sanctuary doors as we waited for our musical cue to enter. "Oh, Sugar Sherry, you look so pretty," he said endearingly. Ever since I was a little girl, he had always called me his "Sugar Sherry," and he was my "Uncle Tiny."

"Oh, thank you! I can't tell you how long I've waited for this day. It means so much to me that you will be escorting me down the aisle. You've always been like a father to me. You'll always have a very special place in my heart," I said, as tears welled up in my eyes.

"I'd do anything for my sweetheart!" he replied, as he kissed me.

The moment that I had earnestly prayed for had finally arrived. The pastor raised his hand and motioned for the guests to rise as I, "the beaming bride," prepared to make my marital debut down the white carpet that was rolled out through the chapel.

Special friends, l to r, Holly Hildreth,
Holly Stratman, Sherry Frattini and Jill Birlson

As my uncle and I walked down the aisle, I smiled at the many guests who had come to celebrate our special day. I walked past my young nieces as they waved and cheered ever so sweetly, "Hi, Aunt Sherry!" When we approached the altar and Ken's eyes met mine, his baby blue eyes were sparkling with tears. *Thank You, Jesus, for Ken!* I whispered.

"Who gives this woman to be married?" the pastor asked.

"Her mother and I do," my Uncle Harold replied, as he passed my hand to Ken.

When Ken's hand embraced mine, I felt a joyful surge flow through my body. When we walked up the steps to meet the pastor at the altar, my flowing cathedral-length train trailed gracefully down the steps behind me. The sunlight streamed through the stained glass windows and reflected off the glistening sequins and shiny pearls on my off-the-shoul-

Uncle Harold has always been like a father to me

der sheath gown. I wore a beautiful pearl crown sewn with tulle that formed a small pouf at the back of my head. With my elegant crown and shimmering gown, I truly felt like Ken's princess.

Our first year of marriage was absolutely the best year of my life. Ken and I were so happy. We upheld our solemn vow to each other and to God always to have Christ at the center of our marriage relationship and our lives. We strove to put each other's needs above our own, and loved being married.

"I love you."

*Here with my sweet nieces,
Kami and Chanel*

"I love you more."

"I love you most-est."

"I love you best-est."

One night Ken and I were wrapped in a warm embrace on the sofa as we watched the evening news. He turned to me with a big grin and shouted, "I l-o-o-ove being married!"

"Me, too!" I replied with equal enthusiasm.

Ken's favorite chapter of the Bible was 1 Corinthians 13. Shortly after he accepted Christ, he carved a plaque with these verses inscribed in wood. The chapter speaks of unconditional love. Ken's character reflected this rare type of affection: *Love is patient, love is kind. It does not envy, it does not boast, it is not proud. It is not rude, it is not self-seeking, it is not easily angered, it keeps no record of wrongs. Love does not delight in evil but rejoices with the truth. It always protects, always trusts, always hopes, always perseveres. Love never fails. And these three remain: faith, hope and love. But the greatest of these is love* (1 Corinthians 13: 4-8a, 13).

Me and my knight dancing at our reception

I was living a wonderful dream. Having longed for a mate for many years, I would walk around the house and exclaim, "I'm married. I can't believe I'm married!" Realistically, we knew that trials would inevitably come. But we were confident that, together, we could work through them.

Ken loved to surprise me. For my thirty-second birthday, he organized a party for me. I was so elated when Ken presented me with a dog for my birthday gift. My new playful gift, Cheyenne, was a golden mix of Chow and Samoyed. The three of us would go on hikes, walks, and picnics.

Ken and I had been married only five months when we received a devastating phone call from his dad. Ken, who was always so cheerful, suddenly became very somber. He said, "Really? When? How is Grandma?"

Ken's voice began to shake. His arm quivered as he handed me the phone. He rested his head on my shoulder and wept uncontrollably. While embracing Ken, I took the receiver and spoke to his dad. I learned the heartbreaking news that Ken's grandpa had died of heart failure. My heart ached for Ken—his sensitivity could hardly endure the pain.

Ken's favorite childhood memories were of helping his grandpa on his farm, riding horses, driving the tractor, and bailing hay.

Ken had a special bond with his grandparents. The bond reminded them to take every opportunity to show how much they cared. I had also developed a deep love for Ken's grandparents. Because I did not have any living grandparents, I longed for a relationship with them. They were thrilled that Ken was so in love with me. When we visited Ken's family in Iowa, his grandparents insisted that we stay with them.

They made sure we were comfortable in "little Kenny's" former room, still adorned with his posters from the '80's. Ken and his grandpa gave me a personalized tour of the farm; they both beamed with happiness as they remembered their special times together. When we entered the barn, they proudly displayed the retired farm equipment, seasoned with dirt and rust from years of strenuous labor. Ken was excited to show me the tractor and motorcycle that he had ridden in his youth.

For our first anniversary we bought each other mountain bikes, and rode them through the immense and breathtaking canyon of Glenwood Springs, Colorado. We filmed our fun days in the canyon with our camcorder. "It is so majestic," I proclaimed, as I addressed the camera.

"Little Kenny" with his grandpa

Ken panned the scenery, then swung the camera back toward me. "Here we are on our first anniversary. It's been the best year of my life being married to you. I love you!" I exclaimed.

"I love you too, B.B.," echoed from behind the lens.

"Next summer we're going to start building our dream home on our ten acres. Ken wants horses, too!" I added.

"Ye-e-sss!" Ken bellowed.

How often I had longed to be the wife "of noble character" described in Proverbs, chapter thirty-one: *A wife of noble character. Who can find her? She is worth far more than rubies. Her husband has full confidence in her and lacks nothing of value. She considers a field and buys it; out of her earnings she plants a vineyard. She opens her arms to the poor and extends her hands to the needy. Her husband is*

My gallant knight

respected at the city gate. She is clothed with strength and dignity; she can laugh at the days to come. She speaks with wisdom, and faithful instruction is on her tongue. Her children arise and call her blessed; her husband also, as he praises her: Many women do noble things, but you surpass them all. Charm is deceptive, and beauty is fleeting; but a woman who fears the Lord is to be praised.

CHAPTER FOUR

Cancer

Praise the Lord, O my soul,
and forget not all his benefits—
who forgives all your sins
and heals all your diseases.
PSALMS 103: 2-3

*T*he month following our first year anniversary in November of 1994, I was employed as an office manager for a software company. One day I received a telephone call from my doctor. I was expecting his call because he had taken tests on my thyroid. Six years before these tests, my doctor had begun taking yearly exams on my thyroid after small cysts had been identified on the gland through a routine physical examination. My doctor had reassured me that these types of cysts were most likely benign. Solitary nodules are of greater concern because they are more likely to be malignant. Up to now all ultrasounds, needle biopsies, and blood work had proven negative. Now, however, a larger cyst had developed in the front of my neck that resembled a three-quarter-inch marble. It was visible when I swallowed because the thyroid gland moves during swallowing. Ken and I prayed diligently about the test results and felt confident that they would be negative.

The doctor's words were devastating, "Mrs. Jones, I received your test results from the laboratory today. Normally, I wouldn't call you at work, but I know you were anxious to hear the outcome. I'm sorry, but I don't have good news for you. We found a malignant tumor. You have thyroid cancer."

My heart started to palpitate wildly. My thoughts were fatalistic. *Cancer! I'm going to die!* I was speechless.

"Mrs. Jones? Are you okay?" he asked.

"No, not really," I managed to utter through my sobs. "I need to call my husband."

I immediately called Ken at work. He was employed as a liability claims investigator for an insurance company. "Ken Jones speaking. How may I help you?" he said in his professional tone.

A well sprung from inside me; I could not contain the tears. Fear tied a knot in my throat. Gasping for air, I managed to say, "Honey, I just heard from the doctor."

After a short silence Ken coaxed me to continue. "Babe, what did he say?"

"I have can...cancer!" I sobbed.

"Really?" Ken was as surprised as I was, but remained calm. He was always levelheaded in emergencies. "You'll be okay, Baby," he replied, with a slight hesitation. "God didn't bring us together to take us apart."

"Please come get me!" I cried.

When I got into the car, Ken put his arms around me in a comforting embrace. I wept uncontrollably on his shoulder. When I raised my head, I caught a glimpse of him wiping his own tears. He said softly, "You'll be okay."

Ken's presence gave me peace in my heart. I knew he would walk beside me and hold my hand. I felt as if I had known Ken all my life—we were so in touch with each other's thoughts and needs. "Oh, Honey, I love you so much!" I said, as I looked into his teary eyes.

"I love you too, B.B.," Ken replied. "You're a fighter. We'll beat this."

Later that afternoon I called my friend Elizabeth Browning, a spiritual mentor and encourager. She invited me over to her house for a prayer meeting that day. I was so comforted by her prayers and wisdom. She reassured me that with God's healing power, good nutrition, and exercise, I would be okay.

When I heard the devastating news, I wanted to call my mom, but I did not want to upset her at work. When she answered her phone that evening, I sobbed, "Mom, the doctor called me at work today. I have cancer!"

Mom comfortingly replied, "Oh, Honey—really? I know how much that upsets you, but I know that everything will work out well."

"Mom, I don't want to die."

"You won't die. We'll pray. God answers prayer," she assured me.

When I returned to work the next day, I was surprised by my co-workers' response. After I left abruptly the preceding day, the owner of our company had informed them of my news. Although they offered their condolences, their questions alarmed me. One woman asked, "Is it terminal?"

With tears in my eyes, I said, "With today's technology, I don't think so. I guess one never knows for sure."

The questioning continued. "What kind is it? What kind of radiation will they do? Do you think your hair will fall out? Will they cut through your neck?"

It then dawned on me that I did not know the answers to all those questions. *Would I die? Was it terminal?*

I was angry and afraid. From the moment I had heard, "You have cancer," it seemed that my every conscious thought involved cancer and death. Thoughts of cancer gnawed through every task that I attempted at work. When I drove down the interstate, while I was grocery shopping, and even when I was at church, I just could not release the torment. I could neither run nor hide from it. It consumed me day and night. I said to myself, *I'm a Christian, I can't be tormented like this. Oh God, help me! Help me!*

When my thoughts wandered from myself, I thought of Ken. *Oh, Lord Jesus, please heal me, for Ken's sake. I don't want him to experience grief through my death.*

The next week Ken was talking to his aunt on the telephone. In a subdued voice he said, "I have some bad news. Sherry has cancer."

I looked at Ken and saw acute fear coupled with great love in his eyes, as they flooded with tears. I knew that Ken loved and adored me, but what I saw in his eyes in that moment touched a deep chord in me. From that point on, I knew I must remain positive, despite the panic I felt.

I have often heard that "the eyes are the windows to the soul." When I looked into Ken's eyes, I knew he had taken my heartache upon himself. We began to stand firm on God's promises of healing: *Jesus went through all the towns and villages, teaching in their synagogues, preaching the good news of the kingdom and healing every disease and sickness* (Matthew 9:35).

Wanting to do my part in my healing process, I researched nutrition and learned of its healing components. Organic foods, including fresh fruits and vegetables, are free of pesticides and contain live enzymes and antioxidants that fight cancer-causing bacteria and free radicals. I changed my diet, prayed, exercised, and took extra vitamins. I wanted to do whatever I could to get healed.

Ken and I continued to trust God for my healing. We asked the elders of our church to pray for me: *Is any one of you sick? He should call the elders of the church to pray over him and anoint him with oil in the name of the Lord; And the prayer offered in faith will make the sick person well; the Lord will raise him up. If he has sinned, he will be forgiven. Therefore confess your sins to each other and pray for each other so that you may be healed. The prayer of the righteous man is powerful and effective* (James 5: 14-16).

We felt that God had honored our prayers and that He was going to heal me through surgery. As Ken and I waited in the examining room to meet with my surgeon, our anxiety grew. Ken nervously fiddled with some of medical instruments on the counter. I thumbed through a couple of magazines, but their pages were a blurred mix of colors. I could not absorb written words. My eyes wandered up and down, then all around. The room revolved chaotically. I closed the magazine as footsteps outside the door came closer and abruptly halted. When I heard a little jiggle on the doorknob, I convinced myself, *Oh, no! It's time to hear the bad news!*

My surgeon, a tall, kind, distinguished, gray-haired man dressed in a long white coat, entered the room and exclaimed, "Well, hello there! How's my girl?" Smiling, he reached out his hand, then warmly pressed his free hand over our handshake.

I smiled, "Hello, Dr. Liechty. I could be better, I guess?"

"You must be the new husband to this sweet gal. I'm Dr. Liechty," he said, as he gave Ken a firm handshake.

"Hello. It's nice to meet you!" Ken replied.

"You know that you have a special lady there," the doctor said.

"Yes, she is special!" Ken said, as he smiled at me.

"We go back a long time. Sherry has been a favorite patient of mine for what—about three or four years now?" the doctor asked.

"It's been five years," I said proudly.

"Doctor, can you explain Sherry's cancer to us, and the procedure?" Ken asked anxiously.

"Yes, of course. Sherry has papillary thyroid cancer. This type of cancer is usually contained in the thyroid. I won't know if the cancer has spread until a biopsy is performed in the surgery lab. If both sides of the thyroid contain cancer, I'll remove about ninety-five percent of the thyroid. This cancer is very slow to grow, but occasionally it does spread, usually to the lymph system. If so, I may have to remove the contaminated nodes as well," the doctor replied.

"Does she need radiation or chemotherapy?" Ken asked.

"Thyroid cancer is treated with radioactive iodine. The thyroid is the only gland that absorbs iodine. About forty years ago a treatment was developed that is quite effective in eliminating all traces of the carcinoma that remain after surgery," the doctor replied.

"Radioactive!" Ken exclaimed. "Isn't that dangerous? Will she have side effects? Will her hair fall out?"

"The side effects are minimal. Occasionally a little nausea or some dizziness is experienced, but usually the patient does very well," the doctor replied.

I crossed my arms to steady my trembling hands. "I've never had surgery. You hear so much about the dangers of anesthesia or infections and all. Is the surgery safe?" I asked.

"The surgery is quite safe. It's probably more dangerous to drive in your car these days. Of course, any surgery involves some risks," the doctor cautioned.

"What kinds of problems could you run into?" I asked.

"Since we are working so close to the vocal cords, if one were damaged it could result in a raspy voice," he explained.

"Has that ever happened in your surgeries?" I asked.

"No, fortunately, it hasn't," the doctor replied.

"We're planning to start a family soon—within the next few months, hopefully," I said as I smiled at Ken. "Will it affect our chances?"

"No, it shouldn't. Although studies have been conducted to prove whether or not the absence of a thyroid could hinder reproduction, they're inconclusive," the doctor replied.

"Doctor, you said, 'the absence of a thyroid,' so does that mean she doesn't need a transplant? How does that work?" Ken asked.

"That's a good question, Mr. Jones. Instead of a thyroid transplant, a daily thyroid replacement pill is taken orally," the doctor explained.

"How long is her recovery after the surgery?" Ken asked.

"The surgery will last about two hours. She'll stay overnight in the hospital for observation. She should be feeling well enough to return to work in about five days," the doctor said encouragingly.

"How many of these surgeries have you performed?" Ken probed.

"Let me see—probably around three thousand, I imagine," the doctor replied.

"Wow!" I gasped. "That's a lot!"

"You'll be just fine," the doctor said reassuringly.

When we left the doctor's office, I found comfort in Ken's embrace. He said, "Babe, I just know that you'll be all right!"

"Thanks, Honey. I hope so," I replied.

"Man, three thousand surgeries! That's incredible!" Ken marveled.

"Yeah, can you believe it?"

"I watched his hands to see if they were shaky. They were steady as a rock!" Ken exclaimed.

"I feel a lot better now that we talked to him," I confided.

"You're right! He's one of the nicest doctors!" Ken said.

"I know. He's always been so kind and fatherly to me. Once he told me that I reminded him of his daughter," I replied.

After our visit with the doctor, I did not feel as if my condition was a "death sentence" anymore. Knowing that Ken would be with me during my surgery brought me great comfort. Although fear continued to seep into my thoughts, we continued to claim God's Word that I would be healed. I knew that Jesus not only died for my sins but my healing too: *He himself bore our sins in his body on the tree, so that we might die to sins and live for righteousness; by his wounds you have been healed* (1 Peter 2: 24).

My thyroid surgery was scheduled for the second week of January 1995. Dr. Liechty gave me his permission to have the surgery postponed until after the holidays because Ken and I wanted to attend his sister's wedding in Iowa on New Year's Eve.

CHAPTER FIVE

The ICU

I will not die but live and proclaim what the Lord has done.
The Lord has chastened me severely,
but he has not given me over to death.
Open for me the gates of righteousness;
I will enter and give thanks to the Lord.
PSALM 118: 17-19

*T*en…nine…eight…"

The room roared with excitement as the clock got ready to strike midnight. I scanned the room through the hundreds of wedding guests, looking for Ken. Our eyes met as he took long strides in my direction.

The countdown continued, "…three…two…one!"

Ken reached his hand around my back. His fingers danced on my skin and glided through the oval opening in the back of my sequined dress. In unison, the crowd shouted, "Happy New Year!"

Ken's teeth sparkled in his boyish grin. He passionately brought me closer to him as he tilted his head toward mine. Our moist lips met as we stood on the wooden dance floor, swaying to the music; another soft kiss. Wanting to preserve this tender moment in a time capsule, I closed my eyes and gently rested my cheek on Ken's shoulder. I was living a fairy tale romance under the glistening white lights strung from the ceiling.

Three days later Ken and I were planning for our journey back home to Denver. We packed our clothes and carefully assembled our Christmas gifts. How I wish I had known that these would be Ken's last plans on earth. I would have cherished each word, each smile, and each touch of his even more that day.

When I stepped out of the cozy, heated house into the subfreezing temperatures of the Midwest, my face felt numb. A transparent sheet of ice lined the driveway, so I walked carefully to the van. I could see my breath turn to frost in the air. Ken and I snuggled to keep warm in the back seat of the van. His aunt turned around to us and exclaimed, "You two are so cute! You look like Ken and Barbie!" Ken placed his hand on top of mine with a gentle squeeze that said, I love you. I always will.

⚶⚶

Ken squeezed my hand in the dark. The sun was falling behind the dried-out January cornfields as our van approached a farmhouse sheltered by a dense line of trees.

Suddenly, a powerful locomotive blasted from behind the thick windbreak of trees. Within seconds the monstrous beast slammed into the right side of our vehicle. Ken and I, and his uncle, were hurled sixty feet from the van into the blistering Iowa winds.

⚶⚶

Painfully I whispered, "I'm here."

A deep voice rumbled, "She's alive! She's alive!"

I strained my eyes to focus on the men lifting me from the ground. Muffled by the sounds of whirling propellers I silently cried, *Jesus! Jesus! Oh, my God, help me!*

⚶⚶

The next day the humming sounds of a respirator invaded my drug-clouded mind. Squinting, I tried to focus on the five sets of eyes that hovered above me. One by one, the doctors and nurses uttered a sympathetic "Hi, Sherry."

Confused and exhausted, I closed my eyes. *Where am I? What happened?*

In the darkness I felt the stiff, cool sheets tucked around my aching body. *I can't move. Someone tell me what's going on! Why can't I hear my voice? It's not a dream. There was an accident. Oh, God, I'm alive!*

Opening my eyes, I struggled to focus on the blurred silhouettes that moved around the room. *Ken, where's Ken?* I hoped and prayed that Ken was only slightly injured and that a nurse was taking care of him too. *Oh, God, let Ken be okay. Why isn't he here?*

The entire left side of my body felt as if it was embedded in cement. *My leg is so heavy! I can't move my arm!* I could barely move my eyes. Metal pins were drilled through my right leg, elevated in traction. Blood oozed through the wrapped gauze. An octopus of tubes extended from my black-and-blue body. A high-pitched symphony that radiated from the monitor signaled that my heart was beating. Frightened by the pain that pulsated in my throat, I panicked. *I can't breathe!*

When I arrived in Iowa City, the trauma team had worked exhaustively to save my life. My life-threatening injuries included a collapsed lung, internal hemorrhaging, a bruised liver, and a cardiac contusion. I had suffered multiple broken bones in my shattered hip, which had also been completely dislocated; a broken leg, arm, clavicle, scapula, and several broken ribs; a dislocated shoulder, multiple pelvic fractures, a deep jagged gash on my leg, severe lacerations across my knee, and a deeply sliced finger. I was scheduled for an eight-hour reconstructive hip surgery the following week.

I wanted desperately to know where Ken was, yet I was afraid to ask. *What if they say something is wrong with him? Is he hurt badly? Is he alive? Jesus, where is Ken?* My thoughts were out of control. Too much time had elapsed. I still had no answers. *Oh God, help me!* I began to rationalize why Ken was not there; soon a torrent of despair swept over me. *He's dead!*

Moments later Ken's father leaned forward and confirmed my deepest fears. He whispered, "Kenny is gone."

My screams were silent. *NO! NO! HE CAN'T BE GONE! Jesus, I need to see Ken! Ken! Ken! I can't live without you!*

Despairingly I closed my eyes and silently prayed, *Why did this happen? God, please show me one reason!*

Never in my life had my faith been so dramatically tested. As I struggled to understand how my loving Father could allow this horrible tragedy to happen, God spoke to me. The words were silent, but His message of love was explicit. I had heard God's voice in the past and knew that these words were divinely appointed. He said, *Tell my people I am coming soon, and tell them to be good to each other.*

Although I was engulfed in pain and confusion, I felt God's peace. It comforted me. I knew He had a specific plan for me to deliver His message: *Behold, I am coming soon! My reward is with me, and I will give to everyone according to what he has done* (Revelation 22: 12).

God's plan for me to minister to people comforted me, but soon agonizing pain engulfed my body like an inferno and extinguished my tranquility. My body felt as if I had been stabbed with a serrated knife that was being twisted and turned. I cried out to Jesus, *I can't handle this suffering anymore!*

I felt as though I had caught a microscopic glimpse of the pain and suffering that Jesus experienced at the cross of Calvary. I asked the same question that He did when He cried out to His Father, saying: *My God, my God, why have you forsaken me?* (Matthew 27: 46b).

Soon the pain medication took over and I drifted back to sleep. Drug-induced hallucinations and vivid nightmares about the accident occupied every unconscious thought: *Train whistles blared. Strong hands grabbed me from behind. They pulled me through a deep cavernous tunnel. The terror intensified when gates fell and blocked the way out. I uttered high-pitched screams in complete horror. Suddenly, Ken rescued me with his loving embrace.*

The nightmare ceased. I opened my eyes wide and heard the high-pitched ditty of the attached heart monitor. Ken was not there. His embrace was not there. Instead, an antiseptic smell permeated the room. I was alone. I realized I would never again feel Ken's gentle touch or see him on earth.

Attached intravenously to morphine, I was allowed to regulate trace amounts by pressing a release button attached to the machine. Since I was in constant agony, I frequently pushed the button, usually without success. It helped, however, because it gave me some sense of physical control. Pushing the button was the only action I could do on my own.

The day after I was transferred from the ICU, I awoke to my doctors' whispers. *What are they saying? Why aren't they talking to me?* After much silence, I questioned them. "What's going on? Doctor, is something wrong?"

"Sherry, we would like to run some more tests. Your skin has a slight orange color. We want to make sure that your liver isn't damaged. Once we finish the tests, we will transfer you back to the ICU for observation," he replied.

Not liver damage! Oh, Lord, am I going to die? I cried. The fragility of life became crystal clear to me. Each time I closed my eyes, I did not know if I would ever wake up. Consumed with fear,

I would scan the hospital room for one last long look. While thoughts of living battled with thoughts of dying, I would admire the beautiful arrangements of fresh flowers that bordered the room. Ever since I was a small child, I had known that for the believer, death meant an immediate presence with Jesus. My recollections of dying at the accident site also reassured me that death was peaceful; so I was not afraid to die, but I was not ready to go.

One day, though, the torturous pain far exceeded the limits of my human endurance, and broke the last thread of hope I had for surviving. *If I die, I die! This torment is killing me anyway.*

Every ounce of energy I had to conquer the battle that raged inside me was robbed from my will. The gates of my heart were flung open to despair. If demons had directed the scene, inch by inch I would feebly crawl to the rocky peak of an abandoned cliff. I would raise my hands toward heaven and wave a white cloth that I had torn from my bed sheets. As the ragged edges unfolded in the wind, I would surrender and cry out, "Take me home!"

Opening my eyes, I silently cried, *Jesus!* Instantly the room was filled with utter peacefulness. Gazing at the ceiling tiles, I realized that the one Word I had cried was the only Word that I needed to conquer the war raging within my soul.

I envisioned the spiritual warfare that battled to seize me, between the demons of wicked destruction and the angelic forces of glorious hope. Demons hovering above my bed whispered despicable lies of despair: *If God is so great, why doesn't He come rescue you? You can't stand the pain any longer. Give up! Die!*

Yet God's armies of angels were steadfastly reassuring me of His power: *Though the mountains be shaken and the hills be removed, yet my unfailing love for you will not be shaken nor my covenant of peace be removed, says the Lord, who has compassion on you* (Isaiah 54:10).

Demonic forces were bound and gagged as the angels triumphantly destroyed them with a mere breath. I felt an overpowering warmth encircling the room, as a sweet floral fragrance filled the air and replaced the stench of despair. An amazing act of God's presence followed: a slight indentation appeared in the sheets near the foot of my bed. Never before had I seen a visible impression that was unaccompanied by a human form. Surprised, I looked again. It was gone! Within seconds another impression appeared on the other side. I knew God's heavenly messengers had arrived. Angels are weightless ministering spirits, but can take on the form of a person. The angels were victorious and took their post near the foot of my bed. When I saw their impressions, I was comforted, realizing God had authorized them to visit me when I was at the lowest point in my life: *The angel of the Lord encamps around those who fear him and he delivers them. Taste and see that the Lord is good; blessed is the man who takes refuge in him* (Psalm 34: 7 & 8).

The right side of the van was completely crushed.

CHAPTER SIX

Mother's Love

I will extend peace to her like a river,
and the wealth of nations like a flooding stream;
you will nurse and be carried on her arm
and dandled on her knees.
As a mother comforts her child,
so will I comfort you.
ISAIAH 66: 12-13A

*O*n the evening of January third the telephone rang, bringing the call that all parents dread. My mom picked up the receiver. "Hello?"

"Hello, Mrs. Henderson?" a voice asked.

"Yes," Mom replied.

"This is Ken's cousin from Iowa. I…I…don't know how to tell you this. There has been a terrible accident. Ken and Sherry were passengers in a van struck by a train."

"What?" Mom exclaimed.

With uncontrollable sobs the cousin continued, "Ken didn't make it. Sherry is in critical condition."

"What? Who is this? What are you talking about?" Mom demanded.

"I'm sorry, but it's true. Ken and his uncle have been killed," the cousin said.

"I don't believe it! Where is Sherry? What hospital?" Mom cried.

Fear tied a knot in Mom's stomach and unbalanced her. She grabbed a kitchen chair to steady herself. *A train? If a car is hit by another car, it's terrible; but a train! They're so powerful and deadly,* she thought.

As she cradled the phone with her trembling hands, Mom asked, "Does she have her arms? Her legs? Is her face cut up? I need the number to the hospital, please!"

After many telephone calls and transfers within the hospital, Mom finally got hold of the doctor in charge. "Yes, ma'am, I attended to your daughter when she arrived in the emergency room. She's in critical condition, has many broken bones, internal injuries, and is on life support, but her arms and legs are still intact. Unfortunately our facilities don't have what she needs, so we're having her airlifted to a better-equipped hospital."

"What? Where are you taking her?" Mom asked.

"We're transferring her to the University Hospital in Iowa City."

"Doctor, please, is she going to live?" Mom begged. Hoping for a comforting reply, the answer was not what she wanted to hear.

"I don't know, ma'am. We won't know until we get the tests back."

"What tests? I want to know now!" Mom demanded.

"Mrs. Henderson, we're doing the best we can. We're trying to stabilize your daughter. We'll know more when we get the tests back," the doctor replied.

"Will she make it, doctor? Please, don't let her die!"

"I don't know, ma'am. I don't know."

Clutching her Bible with both hands, Mom prayed with desperation, "Oh, Lord, please give me strength. I don't believe this! Sherry and I prayed for years that she would meet the man who would be her husband. He was the best man she could have found. When she walked down the aisle on her wedding day, I thought she was going to be taken care of for life. I know You are a good God. There is no darkness at all in You. Oh, Lord, You must have Your reasons, but I'm so numb! You know my heart. Please heal her! Give us strength! I need to be with her so that she won't be alone. I know, Lord, that You are with her right now even as I pray this." Wiping the tears from her eyes Mom walked over to the telephone and dialed her brother's number.

Uncle Harold picked up the receiver, "Hello?"

"I can't believe it! Ken's cousin called from Iowa. Ken and Sherry were in a bad accident. Sherry is in critical condition. Ken and his uncle were killed. The van they were in was hit by a train," Mom sobbed.

Uncle Harold responded, "What? Oh, no, Honey! That's awful! What are they doing for Sherry? Is she conscious?"

"They won't give me any answers. They just say something about tests. My baby, they don't know if she'll make it! Oh, God, I don't know what to do. I want to be with her. I need a plane ticket, but I'm too upset to call the airlines," Mom pleaded.

"Oh, Sweetheart, I'll take care of that. Sherry needs you. It will be good for both of you."

The following day Mom flew from Denver to Cedar Rapids. Settled into her seat on the plane, Mom pleaded with God, "Jesus, please help Sherry to be okay. Help us all, oh Lord."

Hours later I opened my eyes and saw Mom's face for the first time. With both of her soft, strong hands, she gently cupped my IV-pierced hand. Her presence and the warmth from her hands gave me a sense of protection. She smiled and said, "Hi, Honey."

Mom was always an incredible source of strength to me. I knew that everything would be okay now that she was with me. Moments before her arrival I had wanted to die; yet when I looked at her beautiful smile and loving eyes, I thought, *Jesus, Mom needs me. I can't die now.*

When I looked into her face, childhood memories flooded into my mind, comforting me. She was the first person to tell me that God loved me. When I was a child, each Sunday I would wear a beautiful dress, with shiny shoes and sometimes even a lacy hat with ribbons at Easter. When we arrived at church, I would hold Mama's hand and skip into my Sunday school class. Mama's beautiful soprano voice echoed down the halls when she led the songs for the children. As I grew older, our relationship matured into that of best friends.

I knew that Mom had been told about Ken's death, but I wanted to tell her myself. As a small child, my grandmother had taught me sign language. Since I could not talk because of the breathing tubes, I slightly raised my right hand and painstakingly made a "K," then an "E," then an "N." Then I motioned in a soft waving hand,

My family of four, Easter 1964

like a bird fluttering away. She understood. She held my hand and said, "I know, Honey. I know."

Although Mom was incredibly shaken by the tragic news of Ken's death and my critical condition, she faithfully trusted God. I know that God does not value one person's prayers above another, but I feel that a mother's prayers are especially precious to Him. A mother brings her children into the world and has an incredible instinct to care for, protect, and nurture them. God heard and answered my mother's prayers.

As my physical condition vacillated between "critical" and "stable," Mom continued to pray for God's healing power in my life. She called our hometown friend and pastor in Colorado, Brad Strait. He said that within thirty minutes he and his wife Cathy would have sixty people praying for me. Mom wanted all the prayer she could get for me, realizing that more prayer going up meant more power from God. I recalled a letter that I had framed and presented as a gift to my mom when Ken and I were married:

Dear Mom,

When I was a child, you were the first person to tell me that God loved me. I first saw God's love for me through you. You built a solid foundation for our family through your strong faith in God. A household built on faith. You have always been there for me. Your strength and endurance have shown me that when life gets uncertain, God is in control and will never leave us, but will carry us through.

Because I know that a mother's prayers are precious to God, I know that this, my "wedding day," was made special because God heard your prayers to bless me with a godly mate. Thank you for being the best mother for whom I could ever hope.

Mom, I love you!
Sherry

Mom's presence comforted me, but I still struggled to understand why this tragedy had occurred. I wondered whether I had done or said something wrong to provoke God. Still unable to speak in the ICU due to the breathing tubes, I scribbled a note on a piece of paper and handed it to Mom. I asked, "Is God mad at me?"

She gently answered, "No, Dear, God isn't mad at you. I don't understand all of this either, but He loves you."

"Why?" I asked.

"Honey, I don't know why Ken is gone. God's thoughts are so much higher than ours. I know God is good, always. He will work this situation out for good," Mom said, as she picked up her Bible. "Look here, in 1 Peter it talks about trials and how precious our faith is to God: *In this you greatly rejoice, though now for a little while you may have had to suffer grief in all kinds of trials. These have come so that your faith—of greater worth than gold, which perishes even though refined by fire—may be proved genuine and may result in praise and glory and honor when Jesus Christ is revealed* (1 Peter 1: 6, 7)."

I closed my eyes and meditated on the Scriptures that Mom read. *My faith is more precious to Him than gold! What a beautiful analogy of God's love for me!*

Mom frequently read Scriptures to me. They gave me such peace. Mom faithfully came to see me every day in the hospital from eight in the morning until visiting hours were over at the end of the day. She received hundreds of telephone calls from friends, family, and even strangers who heard of the accident and wanted to offer her hope and encouragement. She in turn encouraged them with her faith and belief in God. Mom had the peace that Paul describes in Philippians: *Do not be anxious about anything, but in everything, by prayer and petition, with thanksgiving, present your requests to God. And the peace of God, which transcends all understanding, will guard your hearts and your minds in Christ Jesus* (Philippians 4: 6-7).

A lighthearted moment came when my mom inadvertently called the chief trauma surgeon, Dr. Nepola, "Dr. Napoleon." He put his hand under his front coat panel and declared, "I'm here for my people."

MOTHER'S LOVE

When God selected mothers
He chose from His heart's passion.
Mothers are the Lord's elect
designated from above.

A mother's heart is tender
it's compassionate and warm.
A mother's love is genuine
with rivers of devotion.

I thank God for my mother
whom He selected for me.
She's a virtuous woman
whom I love wholeheartedly.

Sherry M. Jones

CHAPTER SEVEN

Ken's Funeral

Peace I leave with you, my peace I give unto you.
I do not give to you as the world gives.
Do not let your hearts be troubled
and do not be afraid.
JOHN 14: 27

A couple of days following the accident, Ken's family told me that they had arranged a double funeral in Iowa for Ken and his uncle. A hospital social worker knew that I was denied the opportunity to plan or attend Ken's funeral, so she suggested that I write a letter that could be read at his service. I immediately started to pray for God's wisdom. My friends looked up my requested Scriptures, interpreted my scribbles, and wrote my words on paper. In recognition for my love for Ken and our Savior, this is the letter that was read:

> Ken was the kindest, most gentle and tenderhearted man that I had ever known. He treated me like a princess; truly he was a man after God's own heart. Good family values were instilled in Ken at an early age. His grandparents always said that he was a good boy. He accepted Christ into his heart when he was twenty-one years old. Ken was involved in Campus Crusade for Christ in college. He loved God with all of his heart. I prayed for twelve years to meet a Christian man who would put God first and me second. My prayers were answered when I met Ken.
>
> Some of my favorite verses as a child are in John 14:1-3: *Let not your heart be troubled: ye believe in God, believe also in me. In My Father's house are many mansions; if it were not so, I would have told you. I go to prepare a place for you. And if I go and prepare a place for you, I will come again and receive you unto Myself; that where I am there ye may be also* (KJV). These verses have become so much more meaningful

to me. Ken is in his mansion now with Jesus. Please find comfort in knowing that we will see him again. His wish for you, his family and friends, would be for you to ask Jesus into your hearts. John 3: 16, says: *For God so loved the world that he gave his one and only Son, that whoever believes in him, shall not perish, but have eternal life.*

Acts 16: 31, says: *Believe in the Lord Jesus, and you will be saved—you and your household.* Ken and I prayed every night for our family and friends to all believe in Jesus Christ. God sent His Son Jesus to save us from eternal death. It is like a gift. We ask Jesus to come into our hearts. Ken loved all of you very much. He is with Jesus now. He was my precious husband. We may not know why he is gone, but God is a good God. He loves you very much. I love all of you, too. God will keep us strong and He will be with us.

After the funeral, a young relative of Ken's came to visit me in the hospital. With youthful exuberance she described what she had seen at the mortuary. "You should have seen all the flowers and plants! There were rows and rows of them—at least a hundred! There was this huge yellow one that was at least three feet high! Tons of people, too!"

Her young enthusiasm was overwhelming. While I listened to her exuberantly describing the flowers, my heart felt as if it were hemorrhaging. I was dying inside. *I wanted to be there. Ken, my precious Ken, did you like the letter?*

Later that day some friends of Ken's came to visit me and told me about the reception held after the funeral. They said friends and family shared their favorite memories of Ken's life. I was brokenhearted. *Oh, God, why couldn't I have been there? I wanted to hear the stories and share mine, too.* I wished the mortuary would have allowed me a private viewing at the hospital. *I need to see him and say good-bye.* My silent screams went unnoticed. *Ken, I want to bury you in Colorado so I can bring you wild flowers. Nobody can hear me!* I could only lie silently and helplessly with my breathing tubes, still in agonizing pain.

CHAPTER EIGHT

Rise Up and Walk

I say unto thee, Arise, and take up thy bed, and go thy way into thine house.

And immediately he arose, took up the bed, and went forth before them all;

insomuch that they were all amazed, and glorified God, saying, 'We never saw it on this fashion.'

MARK 2: 11, 12, KJV

*E*ach morning before sunrise I was visited by my surgeon and his team of doctors and residents. A bright light pierced the darkness when they entered my room and flicked on the wall switch. "Good morning, Mrs. Jones! How are you feeling today?" the doctor asked.

I blinked a few times to focus my eyes. With the breathing tubes now removed, I sobbed, "Dr. Nepola, I'm in so much pain. I feel like I'm lying on barbed wire. I can't get relief."

"You sustained multiple pelvic fractures, and continuous pressure is placed on your tail bone since you must lay flat on your back," he explained.

"Please, help me," I pleaded.

The doctor scanned through my charts and replied, "We increased your pain medication yesterday. You should be feeling its effects."

I begged, "Please, Doctor! The pain is excruciating!"

He replied compassionately, "Okay, we'll increase the frequency to every three hours instead of every four. That should help to control the pain levels. Ice packs should also help."

It occurred to me that I was unaware of my physical limitations. "Doctor, will I walk again?" I asked hesitantly.

"Yes, Sherry, you will walk again. However, you have much work ahead of you. In a couple of weeks we will start your rehabilitation. Your body will have atrophied from the weeks that you've been immobile, so first we'll get you sitting up. As you progress in rehab, you'll start taking one step at a time, eventually going from the parallel bars to a walker. A couple of months after that you can start to use crutches. Due to the severity of your hip injuries, you cannot bear weight on the right side for several months. Within nine months you should be walking with a cane, most likely with a slight limp," he replied.

Oh, thank God. I can walk again, I whispered.

"One...two...three...lift!" Again it was time for the aides to move me to radiology on the gurney through the echoing corridors, where each small bump or crease in the floor shot arrows of pain straight through me. Once in radiology, I endured seemingly endless cat scans and x-rays. My blood was drawn daily, sometimes two or three times a day. The nurses frequently had difficulty finding a vein for the needle. I felt like an oversized pincushion.

One day Ken's cousin, Lisa, came to visit me, and cautiously entered the room. Within moments I heard a big crash. My eyes moved in the direction where she had been standing, but she was not there. I yelled, "Help!"

A nurse came running into the room, then bent down in the corner and asked Lisa, "Are you okay? I'll be right back!" Within moments two nurses came in, helped Lisa off the floor, and escorted her out the door.

She fainted? I must look scary. Later that day I asked Mom if she could get me a mirror. "You look fine, Dear," Mom replied.

"Mom, please, I want a mirror," I pleaded.

"Well, okay, the next time the nurse is here I'll see if she can get one," Mom said.

"Now, please!" I insisted.

When Mom held up the mirror, an unrecognizable reflection starred back. My flaky skin was tinted orange, with black-and-blue bruises. My cheeks were gaunt from the drastic weight loss—I had dwindled down to one hundred five pounds. Oxygen tubes hung from my nose and rested above my cracked lips. Silver braces reflected from my teeth. Remnants of slivered twigs and dead grass remained in my matted hair, and dark circles ringed my bloodshot eyes. As I stared at the jagged red lines that extended from my blue irises, my grief over Ken's death burned through my soul like wildfire.

Shocked, I said, "I look terrible! Take the mirror."

"Honey, your beautiful face isn't scarred, and you have your arms and legs. The doctor says you'll walk again! Everything will be fine. You'll see," Mom said encouragingly.

Seeing my frustration, the next day Mom brushed and braided my hair and brought some moisturizer and some Chapstick. "Oh, Mom, thank you. I feel so much better now!" I said.

As the days passed, the physical therapy exercises increased. Nausea swept over me as the therapist helped me sit on the edge of my bed. "Okay, easy does it. I'll just have you sit up for a couple of minutes," he instructed, as he helped position my body.

"Oh, Joel, I can't stand this. I'm so nauseous!" I cried.

"Just a couple more minutes today. Next week I'll take you to the rehab center, and we'll work on getting your entire body vertical on the tilt-board," Joel said.

"No, thanks! This is enough torture!" I replied.

"Sherry, it's going to be tiring, but I know you want to get stronger!" he said.

"I'll try, Joel, but I hate this feeling!" I replied.

The next week I was taken to the physical therapy workroom and fastened to a tilt-board. "Okay, Sherry, I'm going to move the tilt-board slowly so that you are at a slight angle. Your feet will be lowered as your head is raised. You may feel some lightheadedness," Joel instructed.

Inch by inch the tilt-board began to move from its horizontal position, until I pleaded, "STOP! Please! I'm going to faint, maybe even throw up."

"Remember, I told you that would be a side-effect. We need to go a little higher," Joel said empathetically. Twice a day the agonizing exercises continued, but Joel was very kind and patient with me. I was thrilled when he told me that I could soon start trying to walk.

The following week I was wheeled to the opening at one end of the parallel bars. The long-awaited moment had arrived! With great anticipation, I sat in the chair and looked down the long barrels of the wooden bars. Two therapists, one on each side, carefully grabbed me under my arms to help me out of the chair. I feebly stood on my boot cast, then placed my hands on top of the smooth sturdy bars and clenched my fingers around them. My legs were so weak that my knees started to buckle, but the therapists quickly helped me to steady myself. I inched my hands down the parallel bars and shuffled forward on my left leg. The weeks of exhausting therapy had paid off—I took my first step!

Two steps later Joel shouted, "Sherry!" My vision dimmed, as if an eclipse had shadowed the light. "Sherry, look at me!" he exclaimed loudly.

"Oh, man, I thought I was going to faint," I replied.

Two steps later, they lowered me back down into the wheelchair. When I returned to my room, I exclaimed, "Mom! I took five steps today!"

"Oh, that is wonderful!" Mom replied.

My journey back to walking again required strenuous effort, but I realized that my mobility was a gift God had given back to me. Mom continued to cheer my accomplishments. She probably had a "déjà vu" moment, one that reminded her of the first steps I took as a child more than thirty years ago.

CHAPTER NINE

Friends Sent To Encourage

*...there is a friend
who sticks closer
than a brother.*
PROVERBS 18: 24B

*T*wo days after the accident as I lay in the ICU, I felt a delicate squeeze on my hand. I slowly opened my pain-filled eyes and focused on the compassionate face of my best friend, Sherry Frattini. *Oh, good, Sherry is here! I knew she'd get here soon! I* thought. Somehow I just knew she would come. We had always been there for each other. We had met at varsity cheerleading tryouts our junior year at Westminster High School. Happily we both made the squad and instantly connected. Still inseparable, we only lived thirty miles apart. When Sherry heard about the accident, she and her husband Mike immediately made flight reservations to Iowa. The accident happened on Sherry's birthday. On that day she had felt a dark cloud hovering above her and sensed that something was wrong.

High school cheerleaders and best friends

Since I could not talk because of the breathing tubes, I feebly motioned for a pen and paper, then wrote, "Ken is dead!"

"I know, Sweetheart. They told me. I'm so sorry. I know how much you loved him," she said sweetly. Seeing the pain in my eyes, she gently kissed my hand and fingers and compassionately said, "I wish I could take some of your pain, so that you wouldn't have to suffer so much." I knew that she meant it.

The ICU was dark, with no windows. Days seemed to stand still, because I could not tell whether it was day or night. A few hours after Sherry's arrival, I opened my eyes and saw her attaching a small digital clock to the bedpost. She said, "Oh, it's so dreary in here. I'll put this little clock here so you'll know that time is passing and this pain will not last forever."

During their three-day visit, Sherry and Mike stayed near my bedside with Mom from morning until night. Their support was invaluable, as they helped me process my fears regarding Ken's death and his funeral. While I slept, they took Mom out for dinner and encouraged her, too.

When Sherry examined my leg that hung in traction, she gasped audibly. "Oh, no! That gash is so deep I can see muscle. Her body is frail and thin, but her leg is swollen like a balloon and is all black and blue, with iodine just poured all over it. Why aren't they taking care of her leg? Please, nurse, can you help her?" Sherry pleaded.

"I'm sorry, but we need to leave it exposed until the doctor decides whether to do a graft or not," the nurse replied.

"It looks so awful and painful," Sherry said. She leaned carefully over my bed and asked, "What can I get for you? Are you comfortable?"

"Please call my surgeon in Denver. My cancer surgery is scheduled for the ninth. Let him know I can't make it," I scribbled.

"Okay, we'll call him. Don't worry," Sherry replied.

"Please make sure Cheyenne is okay. He likes to dig out and I don't want him to escape," I wrote.

"He's safe, Dear. Uncle Harold is watching him," Mom interjected.

Wanting to indulge myself with some lighthearted conversation, I wrote, "While you're here, you can catch some great sights of cows and cornfields!"

Sherry smiled and said, "Oh, yes! It's quite touristy!"

She gently stroked a cool, wet washcloth on my face. *Oh, that feels so refreshing.* "You are a wonderful nurse. I love you guys," I wrote.

"We love you, too! Why don't you close your eyes now and relax. You need your rest," she replied.

I continued to doze on and off. Mike intermittently shared stories of his missionary journeys overseas in Italy and Spain. Enthralled by his stories, sometimes I was able to forget the pain. Shortly after the nurse left the room, I softly moaned. Sherry jumped to her feet and grasped my hand. "Are you in pain?" she asked.

"When they move a pillow—," I started to write.

"Oh, when they move your pillow it hurts you, doesn't it?" Sherry interjected compassionately.

When I started to write, Sherry noticed how difficult it was for me, and tried to complete my sentences for me. My writing was almost illegible, but she patiently waited for me to express my thoughts.

"Are you sleeping okay?" Mike asked.

"Not really. When I get into deep sleep, it's painful, because the nightmares cause sudden jerks. It hurts my back and hip," I replied.

Mom gently rested her head on Sherry's shoulder. "Oh, Sherry, I'm so glad you're here. You have been like a daughter to me. This is so difficult," Mom said, as she cried softly.

"Everything will be fine. God is on our side," Sherry said encouragingly.

They both looked up as a man walked toward them. He asked, "Shirley Henderson?"

"Yes," Mom answered.

"I'm Pastor George Mullen. I have come to pray with you and your daughter," he said.

Sherry said, "See, God is taking care of us."

As I awoke, muffled talk from the television became clearer. It was a story being aired on the program 20/20 about a train. Oblivious to the show being featured, my visitors were in deep discussion. Sounds of deadly screeching metal rumbled off the screen. *Oh, God, a train wreck! I can't watch this—that's how Ken died! I* screamed from within. The IV tube dangled from my trembling hand as I pointed toward the television. Sherry's long brown hair flung around as she caught glimpse of my movement. When her eyes met mine, she captured my fear. "Where's the remote control? Turn that off!" she demanded. Within seconds the picture flickered into snowy waves, then turned black. It was too late. The instant replay was already imbedded in my mind. "Oh, Sherry, I'm so sorry you had to see that," she said.

Before Sherry and Mike headed back to Denver to be with their children, they handed Mom an envelope. "We know that you took time off work to be here. We would like you to have this gift. If my mom was in this situation, I would want her to be taken care of, too," Sherry said.

Mom carefully peeled back the flap of the sealed envelope. To her surprise, she held a generous monetary gift. Mom reached over to hug Sherry and Mike and cried, "Oh, my! Thank you so much. I love you both!"

"We love you, too. God is with you," Sherry said comfortingly.

The evening following Sherry's departure, Mom came into my room and said, "I know how sad you are that Sherry left, but some friends from your Bible study are coming to see you."

A couple days later I heard familiar voices growing closer in the hallway. As the whispers became clearer, I looked up and saw two beautiful blue eyes staring down at me. "Hi, Sherry. We finally made it!" my friend Julie Thulson said, as she reached for my hand.

Intimidated by the machinery that surrounded my body, my two other friends, Jill Birlson and Shelly Dugger, slowly peeked around the drawn curtain and cautiously walked toward my bed. "Hi, Sherry!" they said softly.

"Sherry, we were so concerned about you. We heard so many different stories and rumors about your condition. Now that we're here, it feels so much better just to hold your hand and to see you," Julie said.

I motioned for a pen and paper and wrote, "I'm glad you're here. Thanks for coming."

"Oh, Sherry, we were so worried about you! Before we left Denver, we got together with several friends for a prayer meeting. We asked God to heal your body and your heart completely," Jill said, as she clasped her hands around the bed rail to steady herself.

"We prayed that God would put His loving arms around you and give you peace," Shelly added.

"Oh, thank you!" I replied.

"Sherry, look at all these cards and flowers. You have lots of friends who love you!" Julie exclaimed.

"Is there anything we can do for you?" Jill asked.

I managed to scribble one word, "Pray!" *Oh, Lord, I'm in so much pain! Help me! Please, help me!*

For the next two hours my three friends and my mom took turns praying, reading Scripture, and holding my hand. I was so comforted by their presence. Our reunion reminded me of the many years we had prayed together in our Bible study. Each week we had shared our heart's concerns, prayer requests, and told of our daily happenings. For months my dominant prayer request had been that God would bring a godly man into my life. Then came that unbelievable day when I told the group I had met Ken.

Realizing that Ken was gone only two short years from the time we had met was inconceivable. Devastated by sorrow, I wept in the darkness of the early morning hours. *Lord, where do I go from here?* I prayed. Again, I heard from God. He said, "Write a book!" *Of course, that's it, Lord! I will share my story, so that other people will come to know You.*

Jill's mom, Jesse Birlson, lived near the hospital, and came to visit and pray with me. During her prayer, I felt a subtle twinge of electricity flow through my entire body. God's anointing of hopefulness doused my soul. Jesse had no knowledge of my Word from the Lord, yet God revealed in a prophetic message that I would share my story in speaking and writing. *Thank you, Lord, for confirming Your will in my life.*

Pastor Mullen and a member of his congregation, Tim Breon, visited me often. Tim was a medical student in the hospital. Mom and I looked forward to his daily visits, for he encouraged us greatly. Tim brought Mom a thermos of coffee nearly every day. He and his wife Shannon also made a special Italian dinner for Mom and brought it to the hospital for her.

"I read Sherry's charts. She has extensive damage, especially to her hip, but thankfully she isn't paralyzed. Not only will she walk again, she'll even run!" Tim explained.

"Oh, Tim, thank God. She will run again!" Mom cried.

One day Tim told Mom and me an incredible story about how he thought I survived the accident:

> For many years the angels cultivated the cornfields in preparation for your arrival. They often reclined in the exact spot in the ditch where you were eventually to land. They patiently waited, though at times they got restless. On that fateful day when they saw the train approaching, they had a

*Mom with our new friend and
encourager Tim Breon*

strong urge to intervene, to carry the van up high away from the tracks; yet, they knew it was part of God's plan.

Obediently the angel's wings cushioned your fall. When they caught your head, it protected your mind and face. Miraculously, your spinal cord did not break. The angels wept as Ken's body went limp in their embrace. They cried sorrowfully, but knew his work on earth had been completed, for God softly whispered, "It's part of My plan."

The day following the accident, Mom was in the ICU waiting room when a kind, dark-haired nurse approached her. "Mrs. Henderson?" she asked.

"Yes," Mom replied.

"Hello. My name is Mary. I'm a nurse here at the hospital. I'm so sorry to hear of your daughter's accident. I read in the paper that you're from Colorado. I can't imagine your pain, but would like to help you. We have a lovely guestroom, and would like you to come and stay with us. We can even drive you to the hospital each day."

"Oh, my! Thank you so much, Dear. You're a godsend," Mom replied.

God continued to place people in our lives to comfort and encourage us. One day Mom came walking briskly into my room carrying a huge package. "Look what was at the nurse's station for you. It's from your friend Nina Whyte," Mom said as she cut the tape from the box and brought it near my bed.

When I reached my hand down into the box, I felt something soft and furry. I pulled it out and found myself holding a long-legged white plush bear with a shiny maroon ribbon tied around its neck. Inside the box were other little gifts and a note that read, "I wanted to get you something that you could hug. I hugged all the bears in the store and found the perfect one."

"Oh, it's so adorable! Feel how soft it is!" I said, as I brushed it against my face.

The next day the nurse brought in another huge package. Mom went over to pick it up and said, "It's from your friend Janet Greeno!" Mom excitedly opened the well-packed box. "Oh, my word! Look at all these gifts—it's like a treasure chest! Oh, Sherry, here's a portable cooler with a shoulder strap. It's full of candy and snacks. And here's a lap desk, a cassette recorder, and lots of tapes, too. Oh, wow! Here's a box for me with a lovely scarf in it."

"Janet is so thoughtful, Mom," I replied.

Janet also drove all over town taking pictures of my family, friends, and even co-workers. She assembled these photos in an album and mailed it to me. I was so comforted to see familiar faces. Nina is a talented artist, and painted a bright, cheerful bear on a four-foot card. She and Janet took the card around to my family and friends so they could sign it, then they mailed it to me. It was very comforting to see how many people cared.

"Oh, Sherry, here's a package from Holly Hildreth, and another one from her sister Heather Peters. They're for me!" Mom exclaimed with delight. After she opened both gifts, she smiled and said, "You can definitely tell they're twins. Both of them sent me lovely journals to record my thoughts."

"They have always been such caring friends. They're both so special to me," I said.

All the shelves in my hospital room were filled with beautiful floral arrangements, plush bears, books, and other little gifts. The wall-sized bulletin board was covered with hundreds of cards to encourage me. I was truly amazed by the large volume of calls that came in every day. God blessed me with priceless jewels of friendship during the most difficult time of my life.

JEWELS OF FRIENDSHIP

If diamonds are a girl's best friend,
friendships are truly priceless jewels,
and yours I will treasure forever.
I'm richly blessed to call you my friend.

Your friendship radiates such delight,
a valuable rarity so bright.
Together through laughter and tears,
loyalty is polished through the years.

The radiance of your compassion
illuminates my joyful heart,
for you are God's precious gift to me.
Your friendship is my jewel of happiness.

Sherry M. Jones

CHAPTER TEN

Homeward Bound

Go home to your family
and tell them how much
the Lord has done for you,
and how he has had mercy on you.

MARK 5: 19B

*A*fter thirty long days at the Iowa hospital, the doctor informed me that I could arrange to be transported to a Colorado hospital. It was good news! Yet I had grown comfortable where I was and, strange as it may seem, a part of me wanted to stay.

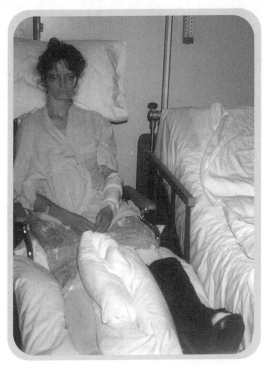

Looking thin, with casts on arm and leg,
but removed from IV's and traction

The staff members were caring, and pain medication was readily available. The thought of re-entering the real world frightened me. I did not want to familiarize myself with a new hospital, to take a jaunt in traffic, to cross over railroad tracks, or to fly in planes. These activities all shared common elements of risk that I did not care to take. In the hospital I felt safe.

My departure resembled a graduation ceremony. Special friendships with the doctors and nurses had evolved during the long days, as we shared stories, dreams, and frustrations. Now the time had come to turn the tassel on my mortarboard, shake their hands, and receive my honorary discharge papers. The good-byes were pleasant, yet painful. I questioned, *Will I ever see these caring friends again?* For a lasting keepsake, they all signed my journal and wrote beautiful, heartfelt sentiments.

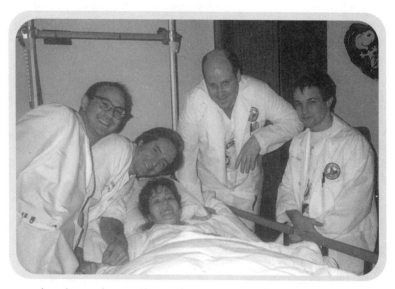

My last day at the Iowa hospital with my wonderful doctors. L to R, Dr. Katz, chief trauma surgeon Dr. James Nepola, Dr. Hopps and Dr. Martin

"You better write to us and let us know how you're doing," Jean said.

"I will. I promise."

"Send us some pictures of you runnin' in that Boulder race!" Mary cheered.

"Sherry, I've never seen anyone with so much faith before. I learned so much from you. Thank you," Jennifer said, as she leaned over the gurney and brushed the hair from my eyes.

"You're a miracle. Don't ever forget it!" the doctor reassured me.

"Thank you all for everything that you did for me. I'll always remember you!" I said with tear-filled eyes.

As the aide pushed me down the hall on the gurney, Mom walked beside us. Suddenly, as we entered the doors of the elevator, an unbelievable feeling of freedom swept over me. *My last elevator ride. Thank God!* When we got out of the elevator, I noticed the huge emergency room exit sign. The same portal I had been whisked through four weeks earlier with little hope of survival, was now the doorway to my emancipation. The automatic double doors opened wide. The abrupt jolt onto the pavement did not even stop my euphoria. *Ahh…air—glorious, fresh air!* The chirping songs of birds resonated in the wind as the cool breeze brushed across my face. I was lying flat on my back, wrapped in blankets like a mummy and strapped to the gurney, but I did not care. I felt free. For the first time in a month, I saw clear blue skies and smelled fresh air.

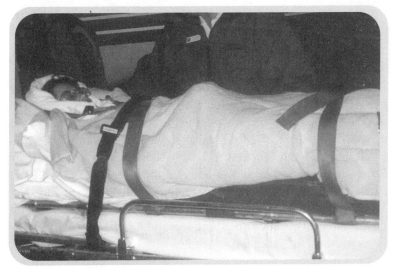

Me wrapped like a mummy but feeling "free."

My heart was pounding when the ambulance left the parking lot. *Please don't let the ambulance driver give me a flying, siren escort to the airport. I don't want any more excitement,* I thought. Fortunately, the driver followed the posted speed limit signs. When the ambulance stopped on the airport runway, the doors opened and two pilots greeted us. Once my gurney was fastened down inside the plane, the flight nurse, Norm, thankfully administered my pain medication. I had hoped for restful sleep, but a short time later into our flight. I was jolted awake by the tumultuous rocking of the plane. *Oh, God, we're going to crash!*

"Hey, Norm, what's going on? Why's the plane shaking?" I gasped.

"Don't worry, Hon. Looks like we ran into some rain," he replied.

"I've never flown in smaller planes. It feels like it's falling apart," I stammered.

"You feel more turbulence in smaller planes. Just relax, we'll be fine," he assured me.

With each jolt of the plane, acute pain shot through my body. I felt as though a handful of darts were being thrust into me. Finally, the turbulence subsided. "Look, Sherry, a rainbow!" Mom exclaimed.

Futilely, I tried to stretch my neck to see. "I can't see it, Mom!" I cried in frustration.

"It's beautiful! I'll describe it to you. The red is the color of a velvety rose, and the orange is almost golden, like a morning sunrise. There are purples and blues that look like a peacock's feathers. God knows how much we love rainbows! I've never seen one above the clouds. Maybe we're the only ones who can see it. God is truly with us. I feel His presence!" Mom said as she settled back into her seat.

It had been dark for several hours when we arrived at Spalding Rehabilitation Hospital. I was wheeled to the third floor, where a friendly, dark-haired aide greeted me. She leaned forward and said, "Hi, I'm Kelly. We've been expecting you. Did you have a good flight? Would you like something to eat?" *Oh, thank God. They're pleasant here, too!* I thought.

The next morning I awoke to a soothing voice of a distinguished middle-aged man dressed in a long white coat. His brown-haired frame towered above my bed as he gently stroked my

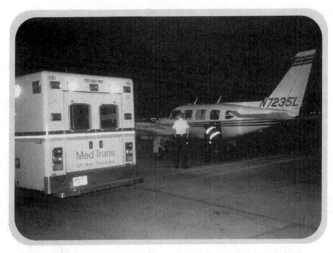

A safe landing in Denver. The airplane that brought us through the rainbow.

shoulder. "Hi, I'm Dr. Goldberg. We'll take good care of you," he reassured me kindly.

"Hi. It's a pleasure to meet you, Doctor," I replied.

"I've been in contact with your doctors from Iowa and have read your charts. You have been through so much. I'm sorry about your loss," he said compassionately.

"Thank you. It's been a difficult road," I replied.

"Your progress seems good at this point. While you are here, we'll introduce you to our occupational, recreational, and physical therapists. We'll help you get back on your feet in no time. Of course, it's going to take lots of hard work," he cautioned.

A few hours later, a lively young woman entered my room. As she stood in the sunlight, golden highlights flickered from her shoulder-length hair. She reached for my hand and said, "Hi, I'm Carrie, the occupational therapist. I'll be teaching you different ways of caring for yourself. Each morning I'll help you dress and show you how to move your arms so you can comb your hair. Eventually I'll show you how to care for yourself when you get home."

The next day I started physical therapy. When I placed my hands on the cool rails of the walker and drew myself to my feet, the room started spinning. I had little strength, but I wanted to work hard. After a couple weeks of therapy, I pushed my walker slowly past the nurse's station that was about fifty yards from my room. When I passed the station, a big round of applause arose behind me. "Go, Girl!" a voice cheered. I felt as if I had completed a grueling marathon.

The recreational therapist organized a brownie baking session. On the way to the session, an aide pushed my wheelchair from behind as I steadied my walker on my lap. When I arrived in the kitchen, the instructions began. "Today we are going to bake brownies. I'll show you how to use the baskets on your walkers to carry your ingredients. You'll learn safe and effective ways to cook and bake for yourself when you get home. Is everybody ready?" Frannie asked.

"Yeah, let's do it!" shouted a spry gray-haired man.

"Okay now, I want everybody to move from your wheelchairs to your walkers and make your way over to the counter," Frannie instructed.

When I opened the refrigerator door, a cool, icy breeze brushed my face as I grabbed for an egg. After I placed the rest of the ingredients into the little wire basket, I carefully pushed the walker back to the table and managed to lower myself to the chair. In frustration, I noticed that most of the water had sloshed over the rim of the cup and onto the floor, as it was half full. The elderly man sitting next to me spoke a few obscenities, as his egg yoke slithered down the sides of his walker. Baking had in the past provided enjoyment, but now was a good day's work.

I soon learned why I was a novelty in the center. "Sherry, we seldom get young people here. Most of the patients are seventy, eighty, and even ninety years old. It's great to have somebody here who's my age. You're a ray of sunshine," Kelly said.

"Oh, Kelly, you are so kind. Thank you!" I replied.

Daily I attended exercise classes with fifteen or more seniors. Our wheelchairs were arranged in a circle, so that everybody could participate. One day I noticed the man sitting next to me surveying my casts. He scratched his shiny head and exclaimed, "Oh, my! What happened to you, Dear?"

"I was in a car accident. We were hit by a train." I said.

"A train!" he exclaimed. "She was hit by a train!" he said to the man sitting next to him.

The room was saturated in silence as the seniors listened intently. As tears flowed from my eyes, I cried, "My husband was killed!"

"Oh, I'm so sorry!" he said.

"That's awful," said another patient.

The class was divided into two sessions—first upper body, then lower body movements. Before session two started, an aide entered the room and escorted a man out of the class who was a recent leg amputee. My heart ached for him. *Oh, Lord Jesus, help that dear man,* I prayed.

I recalled a conversation that I had had with Ken's aunt before I left Iowa. She told me that if I had not been ejected, but left behind in the van, I would probably have lost limbs, since heavy metal had thrust down where my legs would have been. I realized how fortunate I was that I did not lose any limbs in the accident.

The day after I arrived at the Colorado hospital, my Uncle Harold and Aunt Elaine came to visit me. While I was in Iowa, their encouragement had been invaluable, as we had frequently spoken on the telephone. When I saw them, my eyes welled up with tears. "How's my little Sugar?" my uncle asked as he kissed me.

"Oh! It's so wonderful to see you both," I sobbed.

The next day my brother, his wife, and my young nieces came quietly into the room. They hesitantly stood back by the door. When I opened my eyes and saw my nieces, I reached out my hands and said, "My girls are here! Come give Auntie a hug."

Relieved that I was awake, they came running to me and said, "Aunt She-e-e-r-ry."

"Careful, girls. Aunt Sherry is hurt," my brother cautioned.

"It's okay. They'll be careful. I need some hugs," I said.

My six-year-old niece Kami softly put her hand on top of mine and sweetly said, "Aunt Sherry, I made a picture of Uncle Ken in heaven with Jesus and angels. He's happy there."

"Yes, Darling. Uncle Ken is happy with Jesus," I tried to assure her, while I held back my tears.

The next week Aunt Nina came to visit me. "Hello, Dear. How are you feeling today? I got a little something for you," she said as she handed me a delicate green ceramic house that held a little plant.

"Aunt Nina, look at the intricate detail. Thank you so much!" I said.

"My church has been praying for you, Dear. We put your name in the bulletin. Many people have asked me how you are doing," she said.

"Oh, thank you so much for your prayers. I know that God hears them," I replied.

My Uncle Rolland and Aunt Ann came to see me, too. My uncle had been ailing, so I was very glad to see them both doing so well. They brought me a cheery yellow mum to brighten up my room.

When the accident occurred, my brother got hold of my address book and started to call our friends to inform them of the tragedy. The chain was lengthened as each of these friends relayed the information to other friends. During my crucial hours in the ICU, people sometimes called for updates. At that point, the doctors were not certain of the severity of my internal bleeding or of my chances for survival. Since the news traveled eight hundred miles from Iowa to Colorado, some details got jumbled. Rumors spread that I had internal organs removed, had lost limbs, had a completely crushed pelvis, had brain damage, and had even died. Understandably, when first-time visitors arrived they were often very cautious, and would lightly tap on the door.

"Come in," I would say.

Slowly their heads would peer around the corner of the door. They would move a little closer to my bed as they observed their surroundings. Relieved that I was recognizable, they often said, "You look good!"

Much to their surprise, my face was not scarred, my limbs were all intact, and I was not attached to machinery. As often happens following a tragedy, most of our initial conversations were very light. We focused on the weather, hospital food, their jobs, or other safe subjects. I wanted to talk about Ken, and they probably did, too; but generally we seemed to sidestep any mention of the accident. I sensed that when I laughed or even smiled, tensions were relieved, so I tried to remain positive.

Some visitors brought their children and babies into the room. *I want a baby!* I agonized. Husbands and wives would come into the room, then leave together hand in hand. *Oh, Ken, I need you! Why did you leave so early?* Visitors walked freely, without assistance. I so envied them. *Oh, God, this isn't fair!*

Many of my faithful friends came daily to encourage me. Again, all of the shelves in the room were filled with fresh flowers, thriving plants, little angels, plush animals, and cards. I had fifteen visitors on Valentine's Day. My friends knew how difficult being alone would be for me, so they surprised me with a little party in my room. They decorated the room with bright red, pink, and white streamers. Red plastic hearts dangled from the ceiling. In the weeks that followed, we also had a pizza party, as well as a dessert party with Blizzards from Dairy Queen. It was a welcome change from the hospital food.

Two months after the accident, on a cool March day, I was released from the rehabilitation center. Just as at the Iowa hospital, I had developed lasting friendships with the doctors and nurses. One of my favorite nurses came into my room and handed me a little gift wrapped in pink floral paper with a white ribbon tied around it. When I opened the package, it was a cute little stained glass angel. "I heard you like angels, so I wanted you to have it," she said.

"Oh, Judy, it's so beautiful! Thank you so much!" I exclaimed.

A short time later my doctor and several nurses gathered around my bed. "We have a good-bye gift for you," Frannie said, as she handed me a box.

Excitedly I opened the package, and pulled out a large maroon Spalding T-shirt. Each staff member had signed it with sincere wishes in colorful puff-paint. "This is great! I'll remember you each time I wear it. Thank you!" I said.

A few days earlier, Melissa, the physical therapist, had come into my room and exclaimed, "You won't believe it! Last night I was driving down the street, and I turned around and saw this woman roller-blading. She looked exactly like you!" I laughed when I read Melissa's message on the T-shirt: "See you roller-blading!"

Dr. Goldberg had faithfully visited me daily. He was so sincere and caring. "Please come visit us. We'd love to know how you are doing," he said warmly.

Dr. Sheldon Goldberg

"I will. Thank you so much for everything," I said as we hugged good-bye.

I wanted to regain some type of normalcy in my life, but was afraid of what surprises might be looming outside the hospital doors. *I don't want to stay here, but I don't want to go home, either. Ken isn't there. It's going to be so empty,* I reasoned.

CHAPTER ELEVEN

Our House

Therefore everyone who hears these words of mine
and puts them into practice is like a wise man
who built his house on the rock.
The rain came down, the streams rose,
and the winds blew and beat against the house;
yet it did not fall, because it had its
foundation on the rock.
MATTHEW 7: 24, 25

*U*ncle Harold and Aunt Elaine picked me up from the hospital. As we traveled down the road, I envisioned how our house had looked when Ken and I had celebrated Christmas only days before the accident. The Christmas tree had stood tall as the lights twinkled, the garlands glistened, and the ornaments hung from the fanned-out branches. Ken and I had started our first family tradition by collecting a special ornament for each year. Our Christmas gifts, of which my most cherished was a pine jewelry box engraved with intricate details and shiny miniature brass handles that Ken had given to me, were displayed around the base of the tree. Christmas melodies had echoed from the stereo, while the snap of the crackling fire had enhanced the air of serenity. Our favorite enlarged wedding photograph of Ken and me dancing at our reception was placed prominently on our dining room wall.

I recalled the laughter and love we had shared as we opened our gifts. A torrent of tears rushed down my face as I thought, *Ken is gone! I'll never hug him again!*

Before I came home from the hospital, I asked my mom if she would take down the pictures of Ken and me. I also asked my uncle if he could take down the Christmas tree. I knew that in my distressed state of mind, I could not deal with Ken's loss if constantly reminded of the wonderful memories. The occupational therapist had recommended that I have a mechanical hospital bed delivered to my house due to the extent of my injuries. I was so thankful that Uncle Harold and my friend Larry Kindred had taken care of these arrangements for me.

When we drove through our neighborhood, we saw a new restaurant. Since two months had passed since the accident, the seasons had also changed, and now the sun was shining brightly. While my life had seemingly stood still in the hospital, everyone else's lives had gone on. When we pulled into the driveway of our home, the first thing I saw was the young aspen trees that Ken and I had planted the previous summer. Everything I looked at had memories attached to it. *Oh, Ken, remember when we planted that velvety little rose bush?*

Our first Christmas together.

My uncle helped me out of the car as he had been instructed to do by the physical therapist. I grabbed for my walker and slowly climbed the slope of our driveway. An eerie feeling swept over me when I noticed Ken's jeep parked behind the fence. *Oh, God, Ken is gone, but his jeep is still here! He loved that jeep!* It seemed strange that Ken's possessions remained, though he was gone. *Oh, Ken, what will I do without you?*

Ken standing proudly with his jeep

The door swung quietly open. I entered the kitchen and looked toward the dining room. The Christmas tree was no longer there. Our wedding photo was replaced with pictures of flowers. The room felt so empty. I slowly pulled my walker through the living room to our bedroom. I was heartbroken when I saw that our queen-size waterbed had been replaced with a twin-size mechanical hospital bed. *Oh, Ken, our bed is gone!* I cried from within. I lost my balance as the walker got stuck on the carpet. Fortunately, my aunt caught me from behind. *Why couldn't Ken be here waiting for me? I want him to laugh with me, to take care of me.* I wanted to call out his name, "Ken! Ken! Dinner is ready! It's your favorite meal, lasagna!" Yet I knew we would never share a candlelit meal, a prayer, or a laugh together again.

While I was hospitalized, I needed to survive and heal physically; consequently, my grieving process had been delayed. Once I entered our home, where Ken and I had shared so many happy times together, his loss struck me like a bolt of lightning. It was then that I realized the finality of Ken's death. *Oh, God, Ken is dead! He's never coming back!*

As the days dragged on, I would look at our photo albums and reminisce about our wedding, vacations, and Christmases together. A mound of used tissues formed beside me as they soaked up my endless stream of tears. One day I wanted to look at all of our photo albums, including Ken's early years. We had kept those albums on a lower shelf in our closet. Since I could not bend or bear weight on my right leg or hip, I wondered how I could reach the albums. I leaned my crutches against the closet wall, then balanced my left leg in its big boot cast like a trapeze artist. With my right leg extended straight ahead, I placed my hands on the wall and walked them down it one hand at a time until I made it to the albums. My tears splashed onto the plastic covers on the album pages as I flipped through the pages and saw Ken's beautiful eyes and his smile that exuded his love for life.

I gazed up at Ken's clothes hanging over my head. His dress shirts, suits, ties, sweaters, and jeans were all neatly organized. *Oh, Ken, how I wish you were here to wear that suit one more time,* I thought. After spending nearly an hour in the closet, I wondered how I was going to manage to stand up. I clumsily rolled to my left side, put my hand in front of me, dug the toe of my boot into the floor, and pushed with my knee to gain some momentum. After many unsuccessful attempts, I finally stood up.

Reaching for Ken's blue striped wool sweater, I pulled it from the hanger. The threads stretched between my fingers as I crumpled it in my hands. Raising the sweater to my nose, I closed my eyes and deeply inhaled Ken's fragrance. *Ken! I miss you so much!* I cried. I went from one hanger to the next absorbing his scent. *Oh, God, this pain in my heart is more than I can handle. I'm so lonely! Oh, Lord, where are you?* I pleaded. When evening would come, I would glance over to the front door, wishfully anticipating Ken's return. *Ken, please come home! I'm waiting for you!*

When I started the heartrending task of canceling Ken's accounts and attending to other red-tape issues, I was completely overwhelmed to learn that each transaction required a death certificate. For the first couple of months, I had no inner strength to read Ken's actual cause of death. One day as I held this mysterious piece of paper my eyes cautiously wandered to the line that read: Cause of death—"Penetration to the abdomen and multiple trauma to the chest."

"Oh my precious Ken's stomach was pierced. He was traumatized," I cried. He was only thirty-three years old, the same age that Jesus was when He died. My heart grieved over Ken's suffering but I realized that his pain could never compare with Christ's agonizing death on the cross.

The Heart of a Widow

I saw the face of a young widow,
whose heart was torn and shattered.
She longed to feel the warm embrace
of her husband, only now departed.

Why would the Savior, Who created
a perfect union, allow this fatality?
She couldn't believe God intended to seize
her beloved, before her dreams were reality.

She knew that He was the Great Potter
and she was the Maker's clay.
Still questioning the heart-wrenching pain,
she grieved in deep sorrow each day.

The pain and suffering that seemingly
severed the inner lining of her heart,
allowed for bereavement that caused numbness,
leaving her emotions to be set apart.

She couldn't laugh, nor could she cry.
All that she felt was numb.
The God Who promised her the desires of her heart,
seemed deaf to her plea to succumb.

She then was reminded that her Heavenly Father
could not be shut out of her life.
Nothing could separate her from her Father's love
neither height, nor depth, nor strife.

God is love and in Him is no darkness.
For the Light of the World is never dim.
Jesus paid the greatest price,
taking the whole world's sin upon Him.

He did so because of His love for us.
The pain and suffering He endured
were far greater a loss than one has imagined
so that He could become the Living Word.

So as I look in the mirror, my reflection I see,
of this young widow, smiling with certainty,
"My Jesus, my Redeemer, my Comforter and Friend,
thank you for loving me through the end."

Sherry M. Jones

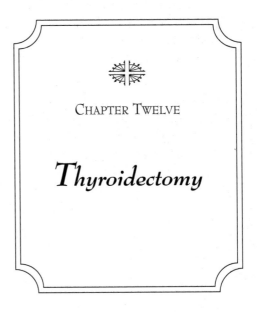

CHAPTER TWELVE

Thyroidectomy

And Jesus went about all the cities and villages,
teaching in their synagogues,
and preaching the gospel of the kingdom,
and healing every sickness
and every disease among the people.
MATTHEW 9:35, KJV

*M*y cancer surgery was postponed until my body was more healed from the accident and subsequent surgeries. Four months after the accident I was scheduled for a complete thyroidectomy. It was a warm, sunny spring day in April. As I walked to the car, I noticed that some lilies in my garden had started to peek out from beneath the hardened soil. I had felt a deep passion for flowers ever since I was a small child. Their smooth lacy textures, variety of shapes and sizes, and bright cheerful colors brought me joy. The rose is my favorite flower, with its soft velvety petals so intricately formed one on top of the other. An innocent bud grows into a perfectly formed peak with a rounded base, like a large teardrop. Soon the bud begins to bloom, wafting forth its sweet, aromatic perfume. The colorful blossom exudes utmost confidence as it gracefully stands at attention on its tall elegant stem.

I thought of how these delicate flowers had bloomed despite adversity. Throughout the long, cold winter these dainty flowers had been buried deep within the compacted soil. Covered with heavy snow, they struggled to survive. In God's timing, the sun came out and overpowered the freezing elements that had surrounded them. The warm rays thawed the harsh frost and gave them another chance to blossom and experience life.

I have always enjoyed the four seasons of Colorado's climate. Sometimes a severe winter snowstorm, or even an occasional blizzard, closes down the schools and some businesses. Springtime is always a welcome change from the cold. Flowers emerge and the grass begins to turn green. Restaurants dust off their patio furniture and open their outdoor seating. Fruit stands with large plump peaches, juicy red cherries, and homegrown tomatoes spring up in empty lots along the busy city streets. Children laugh and shout while riding their bicycles or playing street hockey in the cul-de-sacs.

What if the snow fell year round? Things would be very different. The flowers would never get to experience life. They would remain locked away in the soil for no one to enjoy. The fruit stands would be nonexistent. Children's laughter would be muffled through the windowpanes of their homes.

I felt as if I was a delicate flower that had experienced a frosty winter, buried deep within the hardened soil of despair. My trials had pushed me down into the depths of uncertainty. I was not sure if I would ever resurface and bloom.

As my mom drove me to the hospital, we discussed my fears. "Mom, I can't believe I'm having another surgery. I'm exhausted from battling one trial after another," I cried.

"I know, Dear, but it is so important that they remove the cancer," Mom replied.

"They're going to cut my neck open! Mom, when will this ever end?" I asked despairingly.

When we drove into the patient drop-off area, I watched a man helping a lady out of their car and into a wheelchair. The man then opened the back door and pulled out an adorable little fair-skinned girl. Her curly locks of fiery red hair spiraled gracefully to her shoulders. She wore little stonewashed overalls and a cute striped teal green T-shirt. I often wondered what Ken's and my children would have looked like. I had curly blond hair when I was a little girl. Ken had curly reddish blond hair when he was a boy. I thought maybe our child would have looked like this little girl. The man placed the child on the lady's lap and wheeled them into the hospital. *I wonder why that lady can't walk. Why are they at the hospital? Is she sick, too? Does she have a disease? Is it curable?*

My deep thoughts were cut short when Mom said, "God is with you. I will be praying for you during your surgery."

"Thanks, Mom. I'm so glad you are with me," I said.

Mom helped me out of the car, then I adjusted the cool metal crutches under my arms. When we walked into the hospital, the pungent odor of antiseptics permeated the lobby. The scent immediately triggered horrible memories of needles, cat-scans, tests, and surgeries.

The lady in the admissions office started by asking routine questions. She asked for my name, address, date of birth, social security number, insurance information, and so forth. She stumped me when she asked, "Marital status?"

"Hmm…I'm single. Well, I'm a widow." I said, hesitantly. *I still can't believe Ken's dead!*

"Oh, I'm so sorry! You're so young to be a widow," she said.

"Yes, I know."

"When did you lose your husband?" she asked.

"In January. He was killed in a car accident." I said.

"Oh, you sweet thing! That is so sad," she said compassionately as she paused and shook her head. "I guess we better move on. Have you been hospitalized in the last year?" she asked.

"Yes, for sixty days in January and February," I said.

"Oh, dear! You were in the accident, too?" she exclaimed.

"Yes," I replied.

Each time I told my story I had difficulties sharing the details and inevitably would get teary eyed; yet, through the pain God always gave me the courage to share His love. "We're believers in Jesus Christ. I know I'll see my husband again," I said.

I continued to tell her how God was healing me. She sat on the edge of her chair and listened intently. She even asked questions about my faith. When I left her office, I was excited that God had allowed me the opportunity to witness to her.

I hoped that the joy I had experienced by sharing my faith would last through the entire day or even a whole hour, but it was only momentary. As I limped down the long hallways, fear quickly seeped back into my thoughts.

I was handed a lightweight hospital gown and a drawstring bag for my personal belongings. Entering the dressing room, I grabbed the edge of the privacy curtain and whisked it across the doorway. I propped my crutches against the wall and slowly lowered myself to the bench. I wore Ken's white Disneyland sweatshirt that day because it somehow gave me a sense of security. Leaning forward, I pulled the sweatshirt over my head, held it in my hands and rubbed my fingers over the embossed writing. I reclined back against the wall, closed my eyes, and held the shirt tightly to my chest. *Oh, Ken, remember our vacation? I need you so badly today!* I softly cried. A few moments later I regained my composure, stuffed my personal items into the bag, and walked into the waiting room.

Painful memories haunted me, as the nurse abruptly shoved the IV needle into my hand.

"Ouch! That hurts!" I exclaimed.

"I can't find a vein!" she replied harshly, as she poked my hand again.

"Yeah, they always have a problem finding one. Could you please not be so rough?" I pleaded.

The physical pain from the needle coupled with the emotional pain of Ken's absence was like a volcano erupting in my mind. I recalled how Ken had planned to be at my bedside for this surgery. *Ken, you promised to be here. Now, I'm all alone. I cannot handle this any more, God!* I screamed from within.

While I was lying on the gurney, Dr. Liechty came into the room and said to me in a fatherly tone, "How's my pumpkin?"

His presence calmed my anxiety, as he kindly reassured me that everything would be all right. I trusted him. He introduced me to the anesthesiologist, and before I knew it I fell into deep sleep.

A couple hours following the surgery, a tall young woman in her late twenties walked into my room and identified herself as a resident doctor. "How are you feeling?" she asked.

"My throat is sore, but I'm doing okay," I said reluctantly, not knowing why she was there. I had the feeling that she was going from room to room because she had some extra time on her hands.

"Have you spoken to your surgeon yet?" she asked.

"I saw him in the recovery room briefly."

"Okay, so he probably told you about the problem that we ran into," she said.

"No! What problem?" I asked.

"Oh, well, I should have him explain it to you," she replied.

"No! I want to know now! What happened?" I asked firmly.

"Well—the cancer has spread to your lymph system," she said hesitantly.

"It spread! Oh, God, no!" I cried.

"They couldn't remove all the cancer in the lymph nodes because of their location," she explained.

"What? Isn't it true that if cancer spreads to the lymph system, it's fatal?" I asked.

"Well, I can only say what the facts are here," she replied.

"So, you're telling me I still have cancer?" I said in disbelief.

"Yes, Sherry, I'm sorry. We just couldn't get it all."

Upon hearing this news, I was devastated. I could not contain my horror. *Dear God, I don't understand this! You miraculously saved me from a train wreck. Now, I'm dying of cancer!* I exclaimed.

I felt as if I had been stomped wildly into the ground by a herd of buffalo, then left in the wilderness to shrivel up and die. Blizzard conditions buried my spirit, my joy, and my hope under the hard winter soil. I prayed, but I felt nothing. A couple of hours later my surgeon came into my room. "Hello! How are you feeling, Dear?" he asked.

"Dr. Liechty, some woman came in earlier and said that the cancer was still in my lymph nodes. It frightened me!" I cried.

Dr. Dale Liechty

"Okay, now let me explain this to you," he said kindly, as he pulled a chair next to my bed. "We did find some cancer in the lymph nodes. I removed about five of the nodes, but the other ones were under your collarbone. Taking them out would not be safe, so I left them. Remember what I told you about the radioactive iodine treatment? It is very effective in removing all traces of cancer that remain after the surgery. Okay! So don't worry, you will be fine."

I knew that God had sent my doctor to encourage me. God heard my plea through the cries of despair and replaced the fear with His peace.

CHAPTER THIRTEEN

Realms of Radiation

*The Son is the radiance of God's glory
and the exact representation of his being,
sustaining all things by his powerful word.*
HEBREWS 1:3A

*E*ight weeks after I had the cancer surgery I was scheduled for a radiation treatment. My hospital instructions were to report to the nuclear medicine department, receive an oral dose of radioactive iodine, then remain hospitalized in isolation for a day or two until I consumed enough water to neutralize the radiation waves.

I could not have any visitors because the waves could contaminate them. I realized that this treatment had been successfully used for more than four decades, but I thought, *What on earth is it doing to my body? I can't have visitors, even at a distance—but here I am drinking this radioactive formula that will be flowing through my veins!*

Besides the clothes that I wore that day, I could not bring anything else with me—no books, money, jewelry, jackets, suitcases, or pictures, because they too could get contaminated, and then I would have to throw them out. I was also instructed not to eat anything after ten o'clock the night before the treatment.

Little did I know when I arrived at the hospital the day of the treatment that it would be the most absurd and chaotic hospital experience I had ever encountered. This, of course, says a lot, considering that I had been hospitalized for more than sixty days following the accident.

I arrived early for my eight o'clock appointment and approached the receptionist. "Hi, I'm Sherry Jones. I have an appointment in nuclear medicine."

"Hmm…what time was your appointment for?" she asked hesitantly as she looked at her appointment book.

"Eight o'clock. I'm a few minutes early," I replied.

"Okay, have a seat," she said.

The air conditioner was on high, and the room was so cold that I rubbed my hands up and down my arms to try to keep warm. Moments later a woman approached me. "Sherry Jones?"

"Yes," I replied.

"I'm so sorry, but the doctor usually doesn't come in until around nine o'clock," she said. "Although you were probably told not to eat anything before your treatment, why don't you go ahead and get some breakfast and then come back?"

"Well, that would be fine, but they told me not to bring anything in with me, so I don't have any money to buy breakfast!" I replied.

"Okay, well, wait just a minute. I need to check on something," she said. A few minutes later she returned. "Okay, everything is set up for you. Go to Eight East and tell them that you are there for your tray of food."

When I got off the eighth floor elevator and turned the corner, I was startled by a huge sign that hung from the ceiling. The bold black letters read, "Cancer Center." It was like hearing the news for the first time. Fear gripped my heart. *Oh, God, I have cancer! I can't believe it! I never thought it would happen to me.*

After the cancer surgery I was given an oral synthetic thyroid replacement to take daily. It allowed my body to function normally, as if I had a thyroid. Before the treatment I was told to stop taking my thyroid supplement for four weeks in order to eliminate all traces of synthetic thyroid from my system. This would allow the radioactive iodine to be quickly absorbed by the residual thyroid cancer cells, thus destroying them.

Besides its main function of controlling the metabolism that converts heat to energy, the thyroid also affects every cell in the body. A malfunctioning thyroid can result in decreased concentration, short-term memory loss, constantly feeling cold, depression, and fatigue.[1] Since I had no trace of either natural or synthetic thyroid in my system, every coping mechanism that I had previously had to rationalize thoughts was distorted.

Emotionally raw, I walked blank-faced toward an oval station where four nurses stood behind the counter. I approached the nurse closest to me and said, "Excuse me."

She glared at me briefly and barked, "Do you need something?"

"Yes...I'm Sherry Jones," I said hesitantly. "I was instructed by nuclear medicine to come up here to get a breakfast tray before they administered my treatment."

"What? Who are you? I don't know anything about that! Are you sure you're in the right place?" she asked gruffly.

"Is there anybody here who would know about it?" I sighed.

"I don't know!" came the reply.

Another nurse overheard our conversation and said, "Oh, yeah, yeah, yeah! Go around the corner to the waiting room. We'll bring it to you."

I reclined in a maroon wing chair in the waiting room and stared out the window. The clouds drifted by in a dreary and bleak sky. My mind felt as dismal as the day looked outside; a dark ominous cloud of despair loomed over my head. The word echoed in my mind: *cancer...cancer...cancer! This can't be happening,* I pleaded.

I read several articles, advertisements, and even the fine print in the magazines scattered on a nearby table. *What is taking so long?* I wondered. Moments later I went out into the hallway and told the nurse that I still did not have a food tray. I glanced at the clock. It was ten o'clock.

An elderly patient attached to a portable IV stood nearby and noticed my frustration. She was very lonely and invited me into her room. She told the nurse to have my tray delivered there. I had no inner strength to stand my ground with the nurses so I agreed to go with her. As we conversed and she spoke of her inoperable cancer, I learned that she was terminally ill. She showed me a shiny brass frame that contained an enlarged photograph of smiling people. "These three here are my grandchildren," she said through her tears. "I know they'll be so sad when I'm gone. I just can't bear the thought!"

"I'm so sorry. My husband was killed in January. I miss him so much, but I know I'll see him again, because he knew Jesus as his personal Savior," I said as I witnessed to her.

I simply did not have the fortitude to say anything more. I was weak and emotionally drained. Moments later my food tray finally arrived. The patient had fallen asleep, probably from the shot that the nurse had given to her during our visit. After I had eaten a few bites of the cold scrambled eggs and toast, I headed back down to nuclear medicine. I looked at the clock, and it was almost noon.

After a three-hour episode waiting for a food tray, still the doctor was not available!

The lobby was unusually cold as I continued to wait. It was one o'clock in the afternoon when I finally saw the doctor who was assigned to administer my treatment. Since it was the first time that I had met with him, he asked more disturbing questions about my medical history, then said, "You'll need to take a pregnancy test."

"What?" I exclaimed. "My husband was killed in a car accident in January. I was critically injured. I loved my husband with all my heart. I have not been with anybody since. I'm not pregnant!"

"Well, I'm sorry to hear about your husband, but you still need to take the test," he replied curtly.

"When I was hospitalized from the accident, I had taken a pregnancy test. It was negative. I am not pregnant!" I said firmly.

Unimpressed, he replied, "It's hospital regulation, Mrs. Jones. You must comply, or we cannot treat you at this hospital."

When the nurse put the needle into my arm to draw blood for the pregnancy test, it felt like a swarm of mosquitoes draining every ounce of life from the emotions that sustained me. She held the vial of my blood in her hand and instructed me to wait in the lobby for forty minutes until they got the test results back. *Oh, God, I can't handle this anymore! Please, let somebody help me!* I prayed. In need of some kindness, I tearfully told the nurse about Ken's death and my circumstances. She sympathetically offered her condolences and agreed to take me to my hospital room. At last, I had found someone who cared!

As the nurse opened the door to my room, I thought it was odd that the light switch on the wall was covered with red plastic. When I took a few more steps into the room, I gasped loudly. The entire furnishings of the room, including the bed, telephone, nightstand, and pillow, were all covered with red plastic that read, "Hazardous." A pathway of white paper on the floor led from the door, to the bathroom, and surrounded the bed. As the nurse gave me instructions, a lanky, dark-haired man walked out of the bathroom with a roll of masking tape. He looked at me and said, "It's probably not necessary that we cover the entire room in plastic, but it's just easier. We're taking precautions so that the radiation waves don't transmit through your pores and contaminate the room. We don't want to come back after you're discharged and have to disinfect everything."

It's just easier to cover the room! Easier for whom? I feel like I have the plague! I thought. I could not touch anything or anybody.

He then added, "Oh, yes, since the sink is covered too, here's something to wash your hands."

I looked at the blue packet he was holding and exclaimed, "That's just great! You want me to use Baby Wipes for my hands!" I said in disgust. And again the thought of not having a child with Ken haunted me.

When the two of them left the room, I burst into tears and buried my head in the pillow. My anger was further intensified when the noisy bag that covered the pillow rustled in my ear. It sounded as if I had laid my head on a loud, crinkly newspaper. I could not even cry in peace! *Oh, God, help me! This is so frustrating! I'm cold. I'm hungry. I'm sick and tired of all this confusion!* I cried.

The nail beds of my fingers were visibly purple; my hands were as cold as ice; and goose bumps covered every exposed part of my skin. Evidently the air conditioner was on a timer, and nobody knew how to turn it off. To compensate for the overchilled room, a maintenance man brought in a floor heater and put it next to my bed. The air conditioner and the floor heater were in use simultaneously. Since the bed was covered in plastic, I had visions of it melting with me in it.

To calm my nerves, I asked for a soft drink. The nurse returned a few minutes later and said, "I'm sorry, but I can't get you a soft drink because you're not admitted yet. I'll bring you one on your dinner tray."

"What? I'm not admitted? What's going on here?" I exclaimed.

"I'm not sure, because I'm new here. Can I get you some lunch or something?" she asked.

"Sure. That would be great," I replied. A short time later the nurse returned, cradling a couple of bowls of food in her hands.

"The people in food service made a mistake and put your food on regular plastic plates and trays. You can only have disposable ones, so I grabbed the few things that are in paper bowls. Where do you want me to put them?" she asked.

I looked around the room and grabbed the pink plastic container that held the "welcoming items." I dumped the contents onto the bed and stretched my arm out as far as I could, as I steadied the container. Then I examined the food selection she had given to me—a piece of bread with a pat of butter, a dry wilted salad, and a piece of apple pie, with no silverware. *Hmm... I wonder what the main course was? What am I supposed to eat this with?* I questioned. Finally I had had enough chaos. Moments after she left, I walked out the door and headed toward the nurse's station to complain. Before I had gotten ten feet down the hallway, I was stopped by the technician from nuclear medicine. "Hey, where are you going?" he asked.

"I'm getting some silverware so I can eat my food," I said.

"No, no, no, you can't do that! I'm going to administer the treatment now. You can't eat for two hours," he said gruffly, as he followed me back to the room. Then he called for a nurse to take the food away.

Dressed in a radiation suit from head to toe, he looked like an outer space alien. With his arms extended, he held a long pair of metal forceps that grasped the vial of radioactive iodine. I hesitantly reached for the vial, then slowly swallowed its tasteless contents. He then instructed me to drink lots of water, to dilute the radiation.

Two hours later I pushed the nurse's button so I could ask for my food tray to be redelivered. Nobody responded to the call. Fifteen minutes later I pushed it again. Still nobody answered. Finally I called the hospital operator. "Hello. This is Sherry Jones. I'm a patient here at the hospital. I'm in room 8313. I pushed the nurse's station twenty minutes ago and nobody answered the page. I can't leave my room because I'm radioactive, so can you please send a nurse to my room?" I asked disbelievingly.

"What? You must be kidding!" she replied.

"No, I'm completely serious! Please help me!" I cried.

"Oh, that's terrible! Okay, I'll call them," she said.

A half-hour later a woman's voice finally came on the intercom in my room and said, "Do you need something?"

"Yes! I do!" I exclaimed. "Why didn't anyone answer my pages?"

"I don't know—I think everyone was away from the station helping other patients," she replied. "What do you want?"

"I would like my food tray back," I said.

Half an hour later a nurse came into my room with a food tray. She noticed that I was shivering. "Are you still cold?" she asked.

"Yes! It's freezing in here!" I exclaimed.

"Wow! This room is cold!" she agreed.

Moments later she returned with a sheet-thin blanket and apologized for the delay. She said, "We were out of warm blankets, so I had to order one."

I was shocked. The hospital was out of blankets!

Shortly after my food tray arrived, they brought me my dinner tray. *This is absolutely absurd. I starved for half the day; now I have two food trays in less than one hour!* I thought. I had to laugh as I realized it was just status quo when my dinner tray arrived with not just one, not even two, but three soft drinks on it! *This is unbelievable!* When I finished my meals, I was instructed to dispose of the entire contents in the industrial-sized waste receptacles that were brightly marked, "Contaminated—Hazardous Waste."

Finally I had taken enough abuse, and called the hospital administrator. The assistant answered and asked to take a message. I tearfully explained the devastating happenings of the entire day. She said that she would relay the message to the administrator and that someone would call me back that day. I never heard back from anyone, so I called back the following day. The assistant asked if I had received her message, and I said no. Later I learned that all my calls were being forwarded to the operator because they said I was not admitted yet. That explained why I did not receive any calls that day.

My new endocrinologist entered the room. "Hello, Sherry. How are you?"

"Not well!" I exclaimed.

I went on to tell him of the day's fiascoes. "That's amazing! I didn't even know that you were admitted until late this afternoon. We needed to perform some tests before the radiation treatment was administered, but now it's too late," he said.

"What?" I exclaimed.

I was aghast, and feared that the inadequate testing might have repercussions. *Oh, no, what's going to happen to my body now?* I wondered.

Later that evening I was talking on the telephone to my Uncle Harold, and he said, "I can't hear you very well, Sugar. Your voice sounds muffled. What's that noise?"

"This day has been a complete nightmare! The telephone, bed, sink, and everything else in the room is covered in noisy plastic!" I exclaimed. In my only act of defiance the entire day, I took the plastic off the telephone. "There, how's that? Can you hear me now?"

"Yes, Dear, that's much better," he replied.

The nurse later stopped by and informed me that my blood pressure was elevated. I thought, *No kidding! After today's circus, it's no wonder!*

Although instructed not to bring anything into the hospital with me, I had concealed a pocket-sized Book of St. John, and decided to read it. I felt like Corrie ten Boom did when she smuggled her Bible past the prison guards in Auschwitz.[2] As darkness fell, I clung to this little Book for comfort. Wrapping the blankets around me, I propped myself up in bed and meditated on the Scriptures. I turned to one of my favorite childhood passages: *For God so loved the world that he gave his one and only Son, that whoever believes in him shall not perish but have eternal life* (John 3:16).

I saw a correlation between the radiation treatment that cleansed my body of cancerous cells and the spiritual cleansing that salvation gave to me. When I accepted Jesus into my heart, when I was eight years old, He cleansed me from my sins that could have caused a cancerous growth to form around my heart, mind, and soul. If left unconfessed, the sins could have led to hard-heartedness, bitterness, and eternal damnation. "Oh, Father, this day has been such a mess! Please forgive me for my impatience and my anger. Thank You for cleansing my soul. Thank You, Jesus!" I prayed.

I rejoiced that my sins were washed away through Jesus' blood shed at Calvary: *Wash me, and I shall be whiter than snow. Make me to hear joy and gladness; that the bones which thou hast broken may rejoice* (Psalm 51:7, KJV).

The next day the man from nuclear medicine came in with a hand-held device and waved it in front of me to test the levels of radioactivity in my system. Fortunately, because of the gallons of water I had consumed, the radiation waves were at a safe level and I could be discharged. "Hallelujah! I'm free to leave!" I shouted as I walked out the door. Yes, indeed! Free at last! *So if the Son sets you free, you will be free indeed* (John 8:36).

CHAPTER FOURTEEN

Celebrate Ken

Therefore the redeemed of the Lord shall return,
and come with singing unto Zion;
and everlasting joy shall be upon their head:
they shall obtain gladness and joy;
and sorrow and mourning shall flee away.
ISAIAH 51:11, KJV

Shortly after I arrived home from the radiation treatment, I received a package from Ken's aunt that contained two video-tapes and some pictures. The label on the first tape read, "New Year's Eve Wedding." I remembered Ken had spoken on the tape, so I fast-forwarded it to Ken's brief interview. *Oh, there is my precious Ken,* I thought. He was so handsome in his tailored double-breasted navy suit. On the tape, he encouraged his sister and her new husband to keep Christ in the center of their lives. He wished them a happy marriage like the one we had. I viewed Ken's talk again and again.

When I read the label on the second tape, I burst into tears. It read, "Kenny's Funeral." *Oh, Dear Lord, please give me strength to watch this,* I prayed. My hands were trembling as I inserted the tape into the VCR. The narrator entered a large room in the mortuary that looked like a thriving green house. It was filled with hundreds of plants and elaborate floral arrangements. He even told who had sent some of them. My heart raced as I noticed the camera getting closer and closer to Ken's and his uncle's caskets positioned in a "V" shape near the front of the room. The camera zoomed in on Ken's loving face, now chalky white and puffy. His bruised body was nestled in the casket's white satin lining. "Oh, Ken, my precious Ken," I cried.

When the camera started to pan away, I noticed an enlarged framed Christmas photo of Ken and me propped up in the casket next to his shoulder. The camera stood still and focused on my prince, dressed in his navy suit.

When the camera scanned the audience at the funeral, I noticed that someone else filled the seat near the center aisle that was most often reserved for the grieving widow. I felt so cheated. *Hey, that's my seat! I'm the widow! Oh, Ken, I'm so sorry I wasn't there.* I cried. When the service ended, people walked forward row by row to view his body.

I was devastated that I had been unable to attend Ken's funeral and desperately needed an avenue to grieve his death. A recurring thought continued to run through my mind: *What about a "Celebration Service" for Ken?* I did not want a service with a casket and a hearse, but a service to celebrate Ken's life and his homecoming. I still needed to say good-bye, and I knew our friends did, too. We needed to share our joyful memories of Ken's life. Most important, I wanted God to be glorified.

The plans for the celebration service came together beautifully. I was honored that my friend, Pastor Brad Strait, agreed to officiate at the service. I had a professional video created that showed still pictures of Ken when he was a child, of our engagement, and even some from our wedding video. The video also contained a news segment from the night of the accident.

My friend Nina Whyte designed an invitation. Her father, Joe Drnec, created a sketch of Ken. On the front of the invitation was a Scripture verse found in Matthew.

"Well done, good and faithful servant... enter into the joy of your Master."

Matthew 25:23, KJV

Kenneth William Jones, Jr.
September 11, 1961–January 3, 1995

In Loving Memory

Inside the invitation read:

> *You are invited to attend a celebration service*
> *in honor of the life of my precious husband, Ken.*
> *Your presence will bless my heart and will enable me*

personally to express my deepest gratitude to each of you
for the prayers, flowers, cards and thoughtfulness
that you have extended to me.

God Bless You,
Sherry Jones

When Pastor Brad and I planned the service, I told him that I wanted to speak of my love for Ken. He admired my strength, but cautioned me to be brief, because memorial services often lead to emotional upheaval.

As I contemplated what I would say at this service, I found peace in walking and talking with God. My dog Cheyenne and I would walk across the miles of greenbelt near our house that surrounded a small pond. As I looked across the pond I caught sight of some frolicking wild ducks. When they came up for air, large water drops danced in the air as they shook their shiny heads. I petitioned my heavenly Father and asked for His anointing at the service, that His healing power would fill the auditorium and that I would not break down in uncontrollable tears when I spoke. God confirmed in my heart that He had given me the thoughts to organize Ken's service. I knew that He would be glorified in its completion.

Nearly two hundred people attended Ken's Celebration Service. Shortly after the service started, Pastor Brad announced that I would join him at the altar. On my way up the stairs I prayed that God would fill my mouth with His words: *I am the Lord your God, who brought you up out of Egypt. Open wide your mouth and I will fill it* (Psalm 81:10).

As I stood confidently before the crowd, I scanned the many loving faces of my family, friends, co-workers, neighbors, doctors, and nurses. They had given so much heartfelt love, compassion, and kindness to me. Incredible peace came upon me. God's anointing was so strong. I knew He saw the broken hearts of His precious children who needed to hear of His great love. Many of them had driven a great distance to attend the service and comfort me. I glanced down at my notes only once, when suddenly I felt the presence and warmth of the Son. The words flowed without interruption:

Good Evening! Ken was the kindest, sweetest, most gentle and tenderhearted man that I had ever met in my life. He treated me like a princess. Our first year of marriage was absolutely the best year of my life. People would come up to Ken and me and say, "Isn't the first year of marriage difficult? There are so many adjustments to make."

Ken and I would smile at each other and say, "No, it's wonderful."

The month following our first year of marriage, I received the most devastating telephone call of my life. My doctor told me that I had been diagnosed with thyroid cancer. I immediately called Ken and was instantly comforted by his calmness. He said, "God did not bring us together to take us apart! You will be okay!" I praised our Lord that I had Ken.

My thyroid surgery was scheduled for January ninth, but on January third we were involved in a very serious car/train accident. My memory from the accident was selective, because I was on a lot of morphine. I opened my eyes and saw doctors and nurses hovering above the bed, but I did not see Ken. I was afraid to ask what had happened, because I did not want to hear the answer. A short time later, Ken's father leaned forward and whispered, "Kenny is gone."

I closed my eyes and began to pray. I said, "Lord Jesus, I do not understand this. I prayed for twelve years to meet this precious man of God. Ken loved you with all his heart, and now he is gone. Please show me some reason why this happened."

I never felt so close to God as I did in that moment. His message of love was explicitly clear. He said, "Tell my people I am coming soon, and tell them to be good to each other."

Jesus is coming soon! Nobody knows the day or the hour, but the Bible is the infallible Word of God, and it speaks the truth. Ken's wish for you, his family and friends, if you have not done so already, would be for you to ask Jesus Christ into your hearts. It will be the best decision you will ever make in your life, for we do not know what tomorrow will bring.

Pray this prayer with me. "Dear Heavenly Father, I pray that You will forgive me of my sins. Thank You for sending Jesus to die for me. Thank You that He arose again and we serve a risen Savior. Jesus, I invite You into my heart today."

If you prayed that prayer, all of heaven, including Ken, is rejoicing, because you now have eternal life. We will be able to see Jesus and Ken very soon. God's promises of the Bible are true. He promised He would be a Father to the fatherless and a Husband to the widow. My father died when I was fifteen years old, so for these past eighteen years God has been my Father. For these past six months God has been my Husband. God loves me so much, and He loves each of you here tonight.

I want to thank my heavenly Father for giving me life. The doctors did not think that I would make it either, but my work for Christ is not completed. Ken's work was complete, so he is with our Master. It is hard to understand why things happen. We may never know the reasons, but we will when we see Christ. I would like to encourage you, too, if you are married, if you have children, whatever relationships you have, family and friends, treat them with utmost respect. Love them, adore them, and be good to them.

In closing, I want to thank my mom, family, friends, and each of you for everything you have done for me. Having gone through this without you would have been very difficult. I love you. God bless you.

Once I completed my last words, I paused to smile at Pastor Brad, then walked down the stairs. I reflected upon what the Lord had just done through me. I praised His name; my voice did not shake; my words did not mix; I did not even cry. God did a mighty work in those few moments as I witnessed His truth and healing power.

After I spoke, my friend Lauri Torpen sang a beautiful song that my friends Brionna and Ralph Neumann had written and composed.

NEVER THE SAME

First stanza

I met you that first time at the church dance.
It was God's perfect will, it wasn't just chance.
I waited twelve years to meet the right man.
And we got married as part of God's plan.
I remember getting lost in your baby blue eyes.
And the memory of you makes me realize that
I'm never gonna be the same because of you.

Chorus

I'm never gonna be the same, because of you,
It's a change no one could ever undo.
You made your mark upon my heart
though we may now be apart,
There will be a day I'll see you once more
when we meet upon that heavenly shore.
I'm never gonna be the same because of you.

Second stanza

We could sit and laugh and talk for hours,
or go out on dates with candlelight and flowers.
No matter how or where we'd spend our time,
You would always increase this love of mine.

Bridge

You're my gallant knight, with a heart of gold.
We were gonna share our lives together and grow old.
You always called me your little princess;
our love was deep, yet had innocence.

Pastor Brad's message comforted me. He included the following excerpt from Max Lucado's children's book, *Just in Case You Ever Wonder.*

But as you grow and change,
some things will stay the same,
I'll always love you. I'll always hug you.
I'll always be on your side.

And I want you to know that…
just in case you ever wonder.
In heaven you are so close to God
that He will hug you,
Just like I hug you. It's going to be wonderful.
I will be there, too. I promise.
We will be there together, forever. Remember that…
just in case you ever wonder.

Pastor Brad Strait and me

Part of the service was dedicated to allowing friends to share special memories of Ken. Alexa Ratzlaff, a friend with whom I had worked, told how she had accepted Jesus Christ into her heart when she heard about the accident and our faith in God. It was then that she realized the fragility of life and wanted to spend eternity with Jesus. I knew that Ken, along with Jesus and the angels, rejoiced, because another soul was saved. Many others shared how Ken had touched their lives as well.

My niece Kami was only six years old at the time, but drew a beautiful picture of her Uncle "Kin," in heaven with Jesus and the angels. My mom had always read Bible stories to my nieces, telling them of God's love. Kami drew a wonderful likeness of how she envisioned Ken's homecoming. She saw him now having wings and very happy. Kami had adored her Uncle Ken. Since he had made her laugh and smile, she knew he would be smiling. Ken's mansion was full of many beautiful stones. Because Jesus was so happy to see Ken, He was smiling, too.

Kami adored her Uncle Ken

I included this drawing in the bulletin that we gave to the guests. I also gave everyone present a Bible. I, too, will always remember that winning smile of Ken's. I knew that he was smiling down at his celebration service. He was God's faithful servant, who had completed his work on earth for Christ.

> *Therefore, since we are surrounded by such a great cloud of witnesses, let us throw off everything that hinders and the sin that so easily entangles, and let us run with perseverance the race marked out for us. Let us fix our eyes on Jesus, the author and perfecter of our faith, who for the joy set before him endured the cross, scorning its shame, and sat down at the right hand of the throne of God (Hebrews 12: 1-2).*

Kin's Mansion with Jesus and the Angels

by Kami Henderson (six years old)

*Kami said, "See, 'Kin' is happy with Jesus and
the angels. His mansion in heaven has many beautiful stones.
Jesus is seated and is praying for all of us."*

HEAVEN'S WINDOW

If a window to heaven were propped open for a moment,
my beloved husband would be smiling down upon me.
I would earnestly listen as he told me about
our sovereign God's unfathomable love; as he said:

My dearest one, my time on earth had been completed.
Heaven is the ultimate place for us to adjourn;
the final destiny of our life's imminent flight.
It is greater than anything I could have imagined.

Heaven is an exquisite palace of joyfulness.
My departed mother can embrace me again.
Grandpa tells those stories I loved to hear as a boy.
I met your father today; always know that he loved you.

We're in heaven, for we completed our course on earth.
Don't ever feel abandoned by the ones whom you loved.
With a decade of faithful prayers I longed for a mate,
then God graciously gave me you, a wonderful wife!

I realize that your tender heart has been broken,
because an ocean of tears are stored in your jars.
Allow our God to wipe your teardrops away gently.
Mourn for me no more, but shout for joy that our God reigns.

I was so proud of you as I heard you speak last week.
Do you know why all the heavens then rejoiced?
Another name was written in the Lamb's Book of Life.
My love, we'll embrace again when we meet in heaven.

Sherry M. Jones

His New Place

Jesus called me to this heavenly place.
As we embraced, He said to me, face to face,
*"To My good and faithful servant, well done.
Enter into your Master's joyful fun."*

As I looked up to the glorious sky
there was a vivid sun ray gleaming so high.
Extending from bright rays of dying love,
I saw His nail-scarred hand reach from above.

That was the great day Jesus called me home.
Since then I've seen your heart is all alone.
My love, grieve for me but a short while,
for soon we will meet in heaven's aisle.

Sherry M. Jones

Ken and me at the Bolder Boulder 10K race.

HEAVEN'S FINISH LINE

My mate and I joined in life's marathon race.
We ran together, till I took a slower pace.
A seasoned runner, he was off to a fast start.
Along the way he shared of Jesus' loving heart.

I knew that my mate was ahead in this great race,
for he had just met our Redeemer face to face.
He completed his course at heaven's finish line,
this race he completed in Jesus' record time.

When I reach God's stadium, there my love I'll see.
The crowds will roar like thunder as he cheers for me.
My love will stretch out his arms reaching for my hand.
There we will embrace, high on heaven's grandstand.

When I look to my Savior's compassionate face,
His loving smile will show His glory and grace.
*"You finished your course in My perfect record time,
My child, My love, our earthly race was sublime."*

Sherry M. Jones

CHAPTER FIFTEEN

Depression

Why must I go about mourning, oppressed by the enemy?
Why are you so downcast, O my soul?
Why so disturbed within me?
Put your hope in God, for I will yet praise him,
my Savior and my God.

PSALM 43:2B, 5A

*A*fter I had spent countless hours planning a beautiful memorial service for Ken, finally it was over, the lights were out, and only memories remained. It was an emotional letdown, as all of my time and energy had been consumed in planning all the details, and now I was idle again. I had too much time to think about Ken's loss. Thankfully, the next week I got onto a plane and joined my friends Mary and Mark Cooney on their family vacation in Ocean City, New Jersey. The vacation was just what I needed to help me get refocused. We stayed in a beautiful condo that overlooked the ocean. The sounds of the ocean's mighty, crashing waves comforted and soothed me. Mary is a godly woman and encouraged me greatly to trust in God's plan, as we shared intimate talks while walking along the boardwalk.

When I returned home, idleness slowly took over again. I realized that although Ken's celebration service had been helpful in filling the void that was created when I missed his funeral, still it was not a cure-all for my grief. Due to the multiple losses that I had experienced, an uncontrollable depression crept over me. I slowly slipped into a tempestuous sea of hopelessness. Every fiber in my being wished that I had the ability to "snap out of it," but the problem was too deep.

A biochemical imbalance existed that I had no emotional control over. Neurotransmitters are chemical messengers in the brain that talk back and forth to each other and affect one's emotions, memory, concentration, and tolerance for pain.[1] The cataclysmic events in my life drastically altered my brain's chemicals. In addition to these biochemical changes, the removal of my thyroid also led to radical shifts in my emotions.

Physical activity was virtually impossible, due to my extensive injuries. Before the accident Ken and I worked out at the health club three times a week, played on the church volleyball team, trained for the Bolder Boulder 10K race, and seasonally hiked and biked. We often experienced the "runner's high," as chemicals called endorphins were released that aided in stress and pain management.[2]

When I left the hospital, following the accident, I was given ten prescription drugs, including painkillers, anti-inflammatories, muscle relaxants, sleep aids, and antibiotics. Any type of prescribed medication can affect the brain's chemicals and create toxicity.[3] I continued to have drug-induced hallucinations and recurring nightmares. I slept a lot; besides having little energy, I think sleeping was a way to escape the pain. I prayed for dreams of Ken and often received them. I yearned to feel his warm embrace just one more time. Each morning a bright sun ray would shine through the opening of the sheer curtains in my bedroom window, but instead of rejoicing in the new day, I lay quietly wondering where to find the strength to get up and face another day without Ken.

The moment I heard of Ken's death, I felt as if half of me died as well. The enormous hole in my heart caused by his loss left me feeling completely changed. Events that had always brought me joy and satisfaction no longer mattered. One day Mom and I met some friends at the church where Ken and I had attended. I looked around the lobby—couples were holding hands, children were laughing, and everyone seemed so happy; yet I was dying inside. It was the first time I had been to church without Ken, and the pain was just too much to endure. We entered the sanctuary and found some seats in the middle of the auditorium. I remained seated during the praise songs, because I did not have enough strength to stand. Hundreds of people were all around me, but I felt as if I were isolated on a deserted island. I sobbed uncontrollably and exhausted everyone's tissue supply in the surrounding area. My mom, friends, and the people behind me gave me reassuring pats on my shoulder, yet the tears would not stop. I wanted to run out of the auditorium and never come back, but that would have meant making my way across the long row of people with my crutches, so I just kept my head down and wept until the service ended. The next three times I attended church, the same thing happened—I cried uncontrollably. My church attendance became waned. Ever since I was a child, I had been in church every time the doors opened on Sunday, but now the pain was too unbearable.

My fears of abandonment started to resurface, and my perception of God changed drastically. The physical and emotional pain that I continued to endure left me completely broken and despondent. For the first time in my life, I questioned God's sovereignty. I could not understand how so much tragedy could happen to one person. I do not know if I was trying to punish God for allowing such devastation to happen in my life, but I limited my daily Bible readings and prayer life. Trusting in God's plan was sometimes difficult for me, because it appeared that He had forsaken me. Fortunately my mom, family, friends, and many faithful prayer partners stood in the gap and prayed for me. Although at times they may have felt helpless, their prayers sustained me.

It was one trial on top of another. I detested surgeries, but I was scheduled for another one—this time, shoulder surgery. I had not been aware of the severity of my shoulder injury until I had regained enough strength to move it. During daily routine activities, such as making the bed or reaching my arm up high for a canned item in the cupboard, my shoulder would painfully dislocate. Thoughts of going under the knife, enduring more anesthesia, and possible complications frightened me. I was not looking forward to three more months of physical therapy, either.

I was scheduled for thyroid scans that were unfortunately intertwined with the first year anniversary of Ken's death. Again, all traces of synthetic thyroid needed to be removed from my system so that the iodine could be quickly absorbed by any residual thyroid cells. Once I stopped taking the supplement, I experienced severe physical and emotional changes. I was at my lowest emotional point since the accident.

My experiences had virtually skyrocketed me to the top of the stress scale.[4] The number one stress, the death of a spouse, was coupled with the loss of a dual income, serious personal injury, cancer, thyroid problems, isolation, upcoming surgeries, prescription drugs, limited quiet time with God, and a sedentary lifestyle. It was an enormous amount of change to endure.

I heeded my pastor's advice and made an appointment to meet with a Christian counselor to help me work through my anguish. My initial diagnosis was post-traumatic stress syndrome. I relived the trauma of the accident repeatedly through tormenting nightmares and panic attacks. One day while grocery shopping, I stretched my hand across a shiny mound of red delicious apples. Suddenly my heart started to race, and the apple fell from my trembling hand. The walls started to move closer and closer together, while busy people milling around the store went into a fast-forward speed. I quickly released my white-knuckled hands from the handle of the shopping cart and walked hurriedly toward the door. As I breathed in the fresh air outside, I felt a wet stream of tears coursing down my face. I got into the car, threw my arms around the steering wheel, and lowered my head. "Oh, Father God, please help me!" I cried.

The next day I drove straight to my counselor's office and exclaimed, "I'm losing my mind!"

Luckily for me, as well as having a counseling degree, she was also a registered nurse. She said that because of the abrupt elimination of the thyroid supplement I had lost all coping abilities. She also reminded me that the first year of grieving a death is the most difficult. I was encouraged that once I started to take my thyroid supplement again that my coping abilities would be restored.

On one of my follow-up visits with my medical doctor, I mentioned that I could not concentrate and was lethargic and irrational. She suggested that I take antidepressants to increase my brain's supply of a neurotransmitter called serotonin that helps to regulate mood swings. At first I quickly dismissed her suggestion, because I felt "normal." I was a survivor and could deal with my circumstances on my own. I had heard many sermons from well-known ministers who stressed the dangers of using prescription drugs for emotional control. They insisted that the drugs were merely a temporary solution and that only God could cleanse the spirit of depression. I learned, though, that depression is not just a state of mind, but a serious illness. I knew that God was the Great Physician and in His timing He would heal me, but I was in great need of an immediate solution. *Oh, Lord, forgive me for not being strong. I need Your strength. I can't go on living this way. I need help,* I prayed.

I spoke with my friend, Jesse, a spiritual mentor, who reminded me that God used prescription drugs for my physical healing and could also use them for emotional healing. The next day I reluctantly had the prescription filled. I struggled with my decision. I held the bottle of pills in my hand and argued, *I can't take these. I get my strength from God. He won't let me lose my mind.* The first two antidepressants prescribed to me did not help. Finally, after three months, I found one that did—Prozac. My counselor supported my decision to take antidepressants and stressed the importance of combining such treatment with counseling.

The counseling sessions helped me to understand that my feelings were normal and justifiable responses to the extreme trauma I experienced. I learned to be patient with myself and realized I was doing the best that I could. When well meaning Christians offered me pat answers to my life's tragedies, not only was it not helpful, their "helpful" advice most often discouraged me. They would say, "Go to church." Or "God won't give you more than what you can handle." Or "It happened for a reason." Or "God needed Ken more than you did." Or "It's been long enough—pull yourself together, pick up the pieces, and get on with your life." *What's wrong with me? I'm trying so hard. I guess I'm not handling my heartache very well after all.* Their comments went on and on and on:

A few months after the accident I was speaking to a man who suggested that I volunteer at the hospital, as he did, because it really helped him to get his mind off himself. He said he might play chess with a fifteen-year-old cancer patient, then go to the neonatal unit and hold a "crack" baby. I thought, *Oh, dear Lord, that's all I need—to go to another hospital and expose myself to bad memories, more death, and babies.* I had always been the perpetual caretaker and encourager, but now I simply had no strength to reach out and help anybody.

Weeks later, I hesitantly attended a friend's baby shower. I was happy that God had blessed my friend with a baby, but I was still grieving the loss of my own baby to love. A lady at the party asked me how I knew the guest of honor, and I told her the story of how we had met through my husband. She responded by saying that she knew of my accident and had prayed for me. After that she smiled and nonchalantly said, "Well, you know, God won't give you more than what you can handle!"

I had just met this woman. She only knew a five-minute synopsis of my life. I could not understand how she could make that statement so matter-of-factly. She had no idea of the pain that I continued to endure day after day. *Oh, Lord, nobody understands the depths of my pain,* I cried. I thought, *If God won't give me more than what I can handle, then where is He? I can't handle this anymore! I'm ready to have a nervous breakdown!*

At a restaurant one night, I saw a former neighbor sitting side-by-side with his wife in a booth. He mentioned that he had not seen "us" in church. Because he said "us," I presumed he had not heard of the accident, so I told him what had happened. When I finished my tearful story, he acted indifferent. He smiled and said, "You still need to go to church!"

I was shocked! He did not flinch or offer any condolences, just nudged closer to his wife and kept smiling. He had absolutely no idea of the meaning of what I had told him about Ken's death. I am sure that this neighbor meant no harm by telling me to go to church—after all, church is where we find comfort—but pat answers are not a solution to grief.

I noticed that certain people found it necessary to compare their grief with mine. A friend whom I had lunch with told me that she had just broken up with her boyfriend. She was justifiably upset; however, since I had just lost Ken a few months before that, feeling empathy for her situation was difficult for me. I was floored when she asked me, "Do you know what it feels like to lose your best friend?"

At that point I could not contain the pain any longer. I lost all my composure, and a flood of tears streamed down my checks. *Do I know what it feels like to lose my best friend? YES! YES! YES! I do know how that feels!* I screamed from within.

The next time I spoke with this friend she again commented about this break up, but now commented that her loss "felt like death!"

Again, I was shocked. I thought, *How can you compare breaking up with your boyfriend to death? You can call him. You can hug him. You can even reconcile with him. I cannot do any of that with Ken. He is dead!* To my knowledge this friend had never experienced the death of an immediate family member; I do not think she fully understood the finality of death. Before I met Ken, I, too, had had my share of broken relationships. Yes, they were hurtful, but that pain was not even in the same league with the agonizing turmoil I experienced following Ken's death.

Another person told me that at least my tragedy was not as bad as a friend of theirs whose wife was pregnant and died, because that friend lost two people and I only lost one. *Excuse me? My loss was not as bad? I "only" lost one person?* Loss is loss, no matter how it is counted.

I met a man who had learned of our accident. His first question to me, with no prefacing condolences, was, "Weren't you wearing seat belts?"

Truly I am an advocate of seat belts! However, I wanted to shout from the mountaintop how utterly insensitive his remark was. Did he hear about the fact that we were struck by tons of steel? A car being struck by a train is comparatively similar to a car running over a soda can. They get crushed![5] Did this man perhaps think that he would have avoided a tragedy like ours through his common sense and reasoning powers?

When others would hear of Ken's death, they often asked me if we had had children. Of course my response was no. Most of these people would then conclude, "Oh, that's good!"

Why is that good? We had prayed that God would bless us with children. I wanted a child who would remind me of my beloved Ken and carry on his legacy. Personally, I believe that if people do have children, they feel they must remain strong for them and that life must go on. For instance, when my father died, my mother tried to remain strong for my brother and me. We needed her. However, since I was alone, I got depressed because I felt so lonely. Granted, not having a father would be hard for our children and being a single parent is a difficult task; nonetheless, I felt cheated that I lost my dream of having a family when Ken died.

I learned that grieving has no time limitations. A man asked my mother how I was doing just months after the accident. Because of his Christian beliefs, she shared with him that I was adjusting, but had experienced a minor setback. He responded by saying, "She should be doing better than that by now!"

I knew that this man had neither a medical background nor had he ever experienced the death of a spouse, cancer, or been involved in a tragic accident. I was shocked by his callous conclusions. He even commented that our family was cursed! I was under the impression that he believed that his family was not only not cursed, but also somehow exempt from this type of suffering. The Bible says, however, that when sin entered the world, the whole world was cursed (Genesis 3: 14-19).

Others commented, "You're young. You can get married again."

I did not want another husband. I wanted Ken to be my soul-mate for life. I guess they assumed that since I was a young widow, I should "get over it" quickly and get remarried.

I am sure that these well-meaning Christians just did not know what to say and were trying to comfort me the best that they could. Maybe they were trying to reassure themselves of their own faith. I wondered if they were really thinking, *I'm glad that I'm not in your situation. I hope you can handle it.*

Many people referred to the similarities of my tragedies to those of Job's in the Old Testament. I was amazed at the advice Job received when he was at the lowest point of his life: *I have heard many things like these; miserable comforters are you all. Will your long-winded speeches never end? What ails you that you keep on arguing? I also could speak like you, if you were in my place; I could make fine speeches against you and shake my head at you. But my mouth would encourage you; comfort from my lips would bring you relief* (Job 16:2-5).

It astonished me when others told me how "strong" I was, as I recalled the countless times I cried my eyes out, day after day, month after month. I recalled the times I told my counselor that I thought I was losing my mind. Some people even commented that if their mate died, they could not handle it. I could not imagine what they meant by that, unless they were referring to suicide or a psychiatric hospital. Despite how horrific my circumstances were, I had no other choice but to carry on. Thank God I never contemplated suicide; but at times I wished that the Lord had just taken me home, too. I did not feel "strong"—I felt incredibly weak.

Although insensitive remarks dug deep into my heart, what hurt me even more were the few people whom I considered friends who simply avoided me. They never called to see how I was doing and never stopped by to say hello. I eventually learned that they did not know what to say, so they just stayed away. That hurt the most.

Oh, God, I know You could miraculously heal me right now, but because the depression lingers on You must have Your reasons for allowing this anguish. Please give me strength to get through it, I prayed. I opened my Bible to one of my favorite chapters in Corinthians: *Praise be to the God and Father of our Lord Jesus Christ, the Father of compassion and the God of all comfort, who comforts us in all our troubles, so that we can comfort those in any trouble with the comfort we ourselves have received from God* (2 Corinthians 1: 3-5). I knew that one day God would restore my ability and desire to comfort others.

I heard testimonials about how God instantly healed people of depression. Church elders prayed and anointed me with oil, but misery still accompanied me day and night. I simply could not "pick myself up by my bootstraps" and get on with life. Emotionally I was at the end of a badly frayed rope, barely holding onto one strand with two very tired fingers.

Whenever I heard the sound of a train whistle, my emotional wounds were instantly reopened with terrifying memories that came back to haunt me. When I was driving and had to cross over a set of railroad tracks, I was nearly paralyzed with uncontrollable panic as my heart pulsated wildly.

Job's description of his countenance was a familiar one to me: *My face is red with weeping, deep shadows ring my eyes* (Job 16:16).

What brought me the most comfort was the presence of my dear family and friends. They did not need eloquent speech or to solve my life's unexplainable mystery. Silence was acceptable. Grieving was shared. At times I wanted to share our favorite memories of Ken. I simply needed to have the support of those whom I loved. They offered no advice or pat answers, but simply held my hand and prayed for me. The most comforting words I heard were, "I'm sorry," followed by a hug that said, "I care," while the love in their eyes said, "I'm here for you." Wonderful home cooked meals were delivered daily from churches and friends.

A couple of weeks after I got home from the rehabilitation hospital, my friend Jill Birlson and the ladies from my Bible study hosted a personal gift shower for me to express their love and concern. They gave me a beautiful coat, clothes, perfume, and many heartfelt sentiments. I was deeply touched by their kindness and generosity.

When I began the difficult task of sorting through Ken's clothing, my friends Shelly and Ken Dugger were there to help me. They even asked their church to designate me as their mission project. I was overjoyed with their thoughtfulness as their youth group helped me with much needed yard work.

My friends Holly and Keith Stratman offered to sell Ken's jeep for me since I did not have enough strength in my legs to press the pedals. Letting the jeep go was hard, because I knew how much Ken had enjoyed driving it, but I needed reliable transportation. Since

Ken's company car was repossessed after his death, I purchased another company car from Ken's former employer, Farmer's Insurance. I was overwhelmed by their helpfulness and compassion, especially that of Tim Lasher, a co-worker of Ken's who had visited me in the hospital and now helped me find a new car.

More than once, I was ready to say, "Forget it, God! I've had enough!" Each time, God gave me a glimmer of hope that kept me holding on: a friend would call to encourage me; I would receive a card in the mail; a television minister would inspire me; or my family would surprise me with a visit. In the midst of my sorrow, I thought God had forsaken me. I later learned that He never left my side. Through His great love and mercy He was maturing me into a woman of integrity.

APPLES OF GOLD

If a fresh, plump apple was
dipped into a vat of pure gold,
it would resemble the gift
that you have given to me.

Your encouragement comes from
the lips of God's dear servant.
Your words embrace my sadness,
lifting my heart from despair.

I will frame your heart's kindness
in large pictures of silver.
Your words so fitly spoken
have divinely given hope.

God's servant so humble,
His messenger so kind;
Your lips proclaim His mercy
that is gold and silver lined.

Sherry M. Jones

A word fitly spoken is like apples of gold in pictures of silver
(Proverbs 25:11, KJV)

CHAPTER SIXTEEN

Walking Hand in Hand

(The Accident Site Revisited)

Yet I am always with you,
you hold me by my right hand.
You guide me with your counsel.
PSALM 73: 23, 24A

After the accident I was transferred to a waiting helicopter, then whisked away. I experienced quick flashbacks, but many pieces were still missing. With little memory of the collision, I woke up the next day in the ICU to hear, "You were in an accident! Ken is dead! You're probably dying, too!" The details about what happened during those crucial seconds, minutes, and hours of my life were told to me by doctors, nurses, and family members. It did not seem real. It felt like an unbelievable horror story that cast Ken and me as the main characters:

> Gathered around the campfire for a ghost story, all eyes were fixed on the storyteller's intent brow. Moonlight beamed while the flaming fire crackled in the darkness. The story began with a loud thunderous roar. From behind the trees an enormous black beast emerged. Stunned, the group yelled, "STOP!"
>
> Oblivious to the commands of the crowd, the monstrous beast raced forward, its powerful force pulverizing whatever got in its way! This demon was merciless. Its archenemies were overthrown, and bodies hurled from the wreckage were left dead in winter's frozen scorn. Stunned by the monster's fury, a heartbroken young lover lay still next to her dead warrior.

I did not recall the black beast or see the devastation of the wreckage. I could not see or touch my dead warrior. In God's wisdom, He allowed some retroactive amnesia to shelter me from additional pain, but now I wanted to know details. Somehow I felt a sense of connection to this piece of ground. I needed answers.

Ken's death and the accident were so different from any other tragedy I had experienced. When Dad died, I had held him in my arms. I saw the emergency team administer life-saving techniques and physically strap him to the gurney. When I attended his funeral, I saw him lying in his casket. It felt real because I experienced the entire ordeal in a conscious, healthy state.

In late September of 1998, my mom, Uncle Harold, Aunt Elaine, and I were invited to a cousin's wedding in Iowa that was only ninety miles from the crash site. Although I had wanted to visit the accident site a year or two earlier, it did not work out. Now the time had come for me to get closure on the accident. My family mentioned that they would like to accompany me for extra moral support. We left Colorado early on a Wednesday morning and planned to visit the accident site on the upcoming Friday.

Two weeks before our departure, I called the Iowa State Patrol (ISP) and was very pleased to learn that the two officers I had wanted to meet with were still at that same station. I wanted to meet with the first officer at the scene of the accident, Sergeant Mike Gritton, and also with Trooper Curt Henderson because he helped in reconstructing the accident through his thorough investigation. The receptionist at the ISP was helpful and said she would inform these two officers of my impending visit. She checked their schedules and said they were both working day shifts on that Friday, and to call when I arrived in town.

A couple of months after the accident occurred, I had spoken to both of the officers who had been so extremely helpful. First, I wanted to thank them in person for all that they did to save my life. I also had unanswered questions about the details of the accident that were causing me much unrest.

Thursday night when we arrived in Iowa, I called the ISP. I was disappointed to learn that Sergeant Gritton was working a five o'clock morning shift that day and had an appointment in Cedar Rapids that afternoon. He was really sorry, but he could not meet with me. Also, Trooper Henderson had just received a promotion and needed to return his uniform to a nearby town. He could not make the appointment either. Knowing I was disappointed, the receptionist did say they could probably find an officer who would take me to the accident site.

Before leaving Colorado I had called the television station that did the original news story of the accident in Cedar Rapids and asked if they would be interested in doing a follow-up story on the humanitarian efforts of these officers. The station was thrilled to do the story and agreed to meet us at the ISP on that Friday afternoon. Since it appeared that the officers would be unable to meet me there, I called the television station and told them. They said they could meet the officers later and would still meet me at the ISP. I had no idea what might happen, because it seemed no one would be there.

The four of us drove into Owelein and stopped at McDonald's. As my mom and I were walking back to the car, we noticed that an ISP car was parked behind my vehicle. We both knew that, because of my uncle's charismatic nature that he would have already spoken to whomever was driving that patrol car. Sure enough, as we reached our car my uncle opened the door and said that he had just spoken to the officer. He had told the officer that his niece was here from Colorado, had been in an accident in that town a few years ago, and was looking for the ISP office. The officer said, "Oh, yes, Sherry Jones. I was the first officer at the scene of the accident."

Due to the size of the ISP, we were very surprised that this officer knew of my accident. A few moments later the officer came walking out of the restaurant towards our vehicle. Smiling, he said to me, "You look a lot different from the first time I saw you!"

Startled, I looked at his name badge, then looked at him. I exclaimed, "Wow, you're Sergeant Gritton. I can't believe it! This is so exciting!" Turning to my uncle I said, "This is the man that I wanted to meet!"

I was completely shocked—first, because I did not think the officer was able to meet with me; second, because we met accidentally in a parking lot. He could have parked his car on the other side of the building, or he could have gone to a completely different restaurant in town, and we might never have seen him. God orchestrated the entire meeting.

The first officer at the scene of the accident, who knew more details than any other officer at the ISP, was Sergeant Gritton. He said that he knew how important it was to me, so he had rearranged his schedule. He was working off the time clock and had sacrificed his afternoon appointment to help me bring closure to my accident. Again, the humanitarian heart of this officer was so evident as he gave hours out of his day to meet with me.

We followed him to the ISP station, where he showed me pictures of the accident site and the demolished van. The details in the pictures were mind-boggling, showing coats, luggage, and parts of the van's interior attached to the coupler of the train. Our bench seat was flipped backward. On Ken's side of the bench I noticed a large indentation from the train's impact, where his legs would have been. I saw Ken's gloves on the ground and longed for the picture to become lifelike so that I could reach inside to grab them. Memories of that fatal night echoed through my mind: *The mighty propellers roared as the senseless questions began. "Who are you? Where are you? What's your name?"*

Sergeant Gritton said he had other pictures that he did not want me to see. I trusted his judgment, but wondered, *Were they of Ken and me in the ditch? Were they pictures of Ken, cut up and in blood-stained clothing?* I just did not know.

Although the details became clearer, for a brief moment it felt as if the accident was not my story, but another person's story that I would watch on the nightly news. I could not imagine surviving that horrible crash. The cameraman and reporter sat nearby, so it was, in fact, going to be a story on the evening news; but now it was a follow-up story of hope, kindness, and compassion. It was a humanitarian story of how these officers went beyond their call of duty. It was my story of how God saved my life!

After Sergeant Gritton explained many details and felt reassured that I was ready to visit the accident site, we got into our cars. He led the way, with my vehicle in the middle and the cameraman and reporter trailing behind. I had often envisioned the day I would return to the accident site. I saw myself walking along the ditch in hopes of finding something tangible that had belonged to Ken—a toothbrush, or anything, I did not care what. After I said a prayer on bended knees, I would construct a small memorial site with wild flowers and a white-painted cross.

Now the time had finally come to actually return to the accident site. As I drove, I felt a colony of butterflies fluttering around inside me. Fear overwhelmed me, and I felt panicky. *Why am I doing this? Can I turn around and go back home?* I wondered what it would feel like to see the exact spot where I had lost Ken.

One request I had failed to mention to Sergeant Gritton before we left the station was that I did not want to cross over the railroad tracks in a car again, even though they were no longer in use. I do not know why, but deep down I may have feared a reoccurrence of the collision. Since the accident site was only six miles away, each time I saw a farmhouse and a row of trees I thought, *Is that it?* Then I would look beyond the house and not see a railroad crossing sign. Another farmhouse would appear, but again it would not be the one. A few miles later, the brake lights on Sergeant Gritton's patrol car shone, and the row of flashing lights on top began to turn. For a split second I became entranced by the hypnotic movement of the lights as they flickered from left to right and back again, repeatedly. Looking to the right, I saw the huge windbreak of trees that I had heard so much about. Trees that were only inches tall in the pictures suddenly loomed big as life. I was astonished at their enormous size—they were twenty feet high and the length of a city block! I exclaimed, "Look at those trees! That windbreak is huge!"

As we passed the windbreak, Sergeant Gritton pulled his car over to the side of the road a good fifteen feet before the tracks and parked. Again, this man's sensitivity was incredible. Although I had not told him about my fear of traveling over those fatal tracks again, he just sensed it.

As I got out of the car, I focused intently on the trees. I was so angry that although they protected the farmhouse from the gusty northern winds, they were also the primary reason why the accident had occurred. I stared almost in a trance as I walked closer and closer to the crossbuck sign that simply stated "Railroad." Anger raged inside me as I wondered, *Where are the mechanical gates and flashing lights?*

In my confused state, I somehow refocused on the trees. I walked toward Sergeant Gritton and exclaimed, "Wow, that windbreak is unbelievably huge! It's no wonder the view was obstructed."

Sergeant Gritton nodded in agreement. I asked him if I could have a picture of the two of us together. After we posed for the picture, he said, "I have something for you to help you get through this day."

Sergeant Gritton and me with the little brown bear.

He then reached inside his patrol car and handed me a darling little brown teddy bear that had a yellow T-shirt on that read, "Iowa State Patrol." I exclaimed, "Oh, thank you so much! It's adorable!"

I did not realize then what a comforting effect that little bear would have on my visit. We walked over to the tracks and stood on the exact spot where the collision had occurred. My mind was a heavy fog of jumbled emotions that were hard to decipher. To think that tons of deadly steel had once bolted down those tracks towards us was frightful, yet there we now stood safely in the sunny autumn breeze.

Sergeant Gritton showed me where the van had spun, skidded, and landed in the ditch. As he pointed toward the ditch, I asked him where Ken and I had landed. We walked closer to the ditch and I noticed that it was deep, like a ravine. Since the seasons had changed, the weather was now warm, a balmy eighty degrees—one hundred degrees warmer than on that fatal night. The snow had melted, and the ground was covered with grassy green weeds. Tall, lanky cornstalks formed a backdrop behind the infamous ditch. I had often heard that we landed in a ditch, but I assumed it was a small irrigation ditch. This ditch was at least five feet deep, and its length extended for miles along the road.

With a tremendous amount of brotherly love, Sergeant Gritton held my hand as we walked down inside the ditch and stood in its valley. I felt a warmth flow though my arm and penetrate my heart, and knew God would guide me through the entire ordeal. There we stood in the exact spot where I had landed, was rescued, then carried off. Sergeant Gritton said that he was there within fifteen minutes after the impact of the accident. The people who lived in the farmhouse had heard the crash and immediately dialed 911. He said that as he had walked toward me that night, his feet at times had crushed the snow beneath him. The snow was only days old, and may have helped to cushion my fall. With tears in his eyes he asked me, "Do you remember somebody saying, 'Everything is going to be okay. Hang in there. You're going to make it!'?"

I smiled and said, "No, I'm sorry. I don't recall those exact words, but was that you?"

Standing in the valley of the ditch where Ken and I landed after being ejected 60 feet from the van

He smiled and said, "Yes." He paused, then continued. "I didn't know your name. I didn't even know your relationship to the other people. The scene looked like a war zone, but I knew that you were alive. I covered you with blankets, knelt down beside you, and told you that everything would be okay."

With my heart full of gratitude I said, "Thank you! Thank you so much!"

Since two fatalities were next to me that night, I asked him, "Did you think that I would survive?"

He responded tearfully, "I knew that you were alive. Where there is life, there is hope."

When he arrived at the accident site, he told me, I was face down, with my back slightly arched up. Several rescuers carried me up to the ambulance in a large basket. I was later transferred on a gurney to the helicopter. Although he had called for three heli-

Walking out of the valley of death hand in hand with Sergeant Gritton. A cameraman is behind us.

copters, he later canceled two of them, because he knew that I was the sole survivor in the ditch.

After we had gone through the details of the accident, Sergeant Gritton again reached for my hand as we walked up from the bottom of the ditch. Those moments held a tremendous amount of significance for me. I envisioned Christ holding me by the hand to comfort me as we walked through the valley of death onto the freshly paved road of new beginnings: *Even though I walk through the valley of the shadow of death, I will fear no evil, for you are with me; your rod and your staff, they comfort me* (Psalm 23: 4, KJV).

On the night of the fatal accident, Christ carried me in His arms. On the sunny autumn day when I revisited the accident site, I walked hand in hand with Jesus and left the unanswered questions behind.

When we reached the top of the ditch, the reporter asked if she could interview us separately. The reporter first interviewed Sergeant Gritton. "Why are you here today?" she asked.

He replied, "I am here today for Sherry, to help her get through this time. I knew how important it was to her and wanted to be here for her."

"Do other people that you've helped in accidents often come back to say, 'Thank you?'" she asked.

He responded, with tear-filled eyes, "No, not really. It's good to see how well Sherry is getting along with her life. I wish I could have done more that night."

When I saw his sincerity and tears, I became teary-eyed, too. I was eternally grateful to him for all that he had done for me. "Sherry, how does it feel to be here today?" the reporter asked me.

"It's bittersweet," I said, with tear-filled eyes. "It's painful, because this is where I lost my best friend; yet I'm grateful, because it's here where God also spared my life."

"Why did you want to come back today?" she asked me.

"I felt that I needed closure. I needed to have questions answered. Primarily, I wanted to thank Sergeant Gritton, the police officers, and the entire rescue team who responded so quickly and heroically to the accident," I replied.

Once my interview was completed, I walked back to the cars with the reporter and cameraman. As Sergeant Gritton and I hugged good-bye, he said, "You're going to be all right."

A river of tears came streaming down my face. I said, "Thank you. Thank you so much for everything you did for me."

He warmly said, "You're welcome."

We hugged again, then turned to walk to our own vehicles. As we drove away, I clenched the little brown teddy bear and felt God's peace surround me, as a heavy burden was lifted that day.

God orchestrated that entire day, from the surprise meeting at McDonald's, to the coordinating of the news station, to the comfort of a teddy bear, to the compassion of a great humanitarian, Sergeant Mike Gritton. God allowed me to meet with the man who could answer every question that I presented to him. Even though years had passed, his recollection of that night remained vividly ingrained in his memory.

To my delight, Trooper Henderson was also able to meet with us, in a town along our way back to Cedar Rapids. We were encouraged when he shared his near-death testimonial with us. He told us of one day when he had been driving his patrol car down a country road similar to the one on which our accident had occurred. Due to the dense fog that day, visibility was zero, and he slammed into a boxcar on a freight train that was traveling forty miles per hour. The impact sheared off the front of his car, but miraculously he survived without a scratch. Opening his car door, he fell to his knees praising the Lord for his mercy. Then he immediately called his wife on his cellular phone and learned that she was praying for his protection at that exact moment. My family and I rejoiced in our Lord's mercy. Ironically, the date of his accident was one day before ours, a few years later.

I then asked him what he remembered about our accident. He said that he had been training a new officer that night. When they approached Sergeant Gritton, they learned of the fatalities. He said it was the worst accident that he had ever seen, and he remembered the weather being so cold that when he tried to document the facts on paper, the ink in his pen was frozen.

The next day we visited the hospital in Iowa City where I had stayed for a month. I was honored that Dr. Nepola took time out of his busy schedule to meet with me. He reminded me of a potter who had formed a delicate masterpiece out of a torn piece of clay. He smiled and said, "Walk for me!" I took a few steps for him. "Terrific! Beautiful!"

"Thank you! Thank you so much for everything you did for me," I said, with heartfelt gratitude.

My newlywed parents. What a handsome pair (1956).

Me and my poodle skirt at two years old.

Shout for joy! Cheerleading my senior year at Westminster High School.

A college Christmas with Uncle Harold.

Ken and me at a friend's wedding. I had a special feeling our wedding would be next.

Our wedding day.
The happiest day of my life.

A very happy mother of the bride.

Uncle Harold was my honorary father and walked me down the aisle. Here with my Aunt Elaine, Ken, me and Mom.

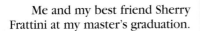

Me and my best friend Sherry Frattini at my master's graduation.

An interview with Ruben and Susan Mendez, friends and co-hosts of Daystar's Rocky Mountain Celebration.

The entire side of the van was ripped off. Notice our bench seat was dislodged off its tracks, crushed, and thrown backward.

Coats and sheet metal attached to the coupler of the train.

He smiled warmly and said, "You're welcome!"

I looked at him and could not imagine the tragedies that he must deal with every day as patients are wheeled through the trauma center. Seeing him again was wonderful, but the best part for both of us was that I had walked through the front doors of the hospital on my own, as a whole and completely healed visitor.

At last all the pieces to my puzzle were accounted for and intact, and my questions were all answered. I realized that, without a doubt, I had survived the collision by the grace of God. He was down in the ditch with me, and He was next to me in the trauma center. He never left my side!

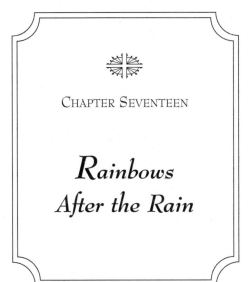

CHAPTER SEVENTEEN

Rainbows After the Rain

*I have set my rainbow in the clouds,
and it will be the sign of the covenant
between me and the earth.*
GENESIS 9: 13

I recall that pivotal moment in the ICU when I asked God to show me *one* reason why the accident occurred. Today, I stand in awe as He has faithfully given me *one hundred* reasons. From my brokenness, I gained greater compassion for those who hurt. I know the many levels of pain that come with multiple losses and depression. I have become stronger and more pliable. The trivial things in my life are not so important anymore, but the value I place on relationships has increased tenfold.

I am eagerly awaiting Jesus' return. How true is the saying, "You can't take it with you!" For what possessions on earth can compare with heaven's grandeur: *The wall was made of jasper, and the city of pure gold, as pure glass. The foundations of the city wall were decorated with every kind of precious stone. The first foundation was jasper, the second sapphire,…the fourth emerald,…the ninth topaz,…and the twelfth amethyst. The twelve gates were twelve pearls, each gate made of a single pearl. The great street of the city was of pure gold, like transparent glass. I did not see a temple in the city, because the Lord God Almighty and the Lamb are its temple. The city does not need the sun or the moon to shine on it, for the glory of God gives it light and the Lamb is its lamp. The nations will walk by its light and the kings of the earth will bring their splendor into it. On no day will the gates ever be shut, for there will be no night there. The glory and honor of the nations will be brought into it. Nothing impure will ever enter it, nor will anyone who does what is shameful or deceitful, but only those whose names are written in the Lamb's book of life* (Revelations 21: 18-27).

If I had not experienced the accident, I could not have shared Jesus with the doctors, nurses, therapists, and receptionists whom I met through the hospitals. Although I already knew how blessed I was with wonderful family and friends, they proved their loyalty in ways I could never have imagined. I gained greater empathy for the weary—when my friend Kay's husband was near death in the ICU from a serious car accident, I could pray with her and encourage her to trust in God's faithfulness. One of my greatest gifts has been to see Jesus through the eyes of a child. When children ask me why I do not have any kids, a husband, or a daddy to take care of me, I say that Jesus is my Daddy and provides my every need. He is my Abba Father (Romans 8:15).

In God's great plan of restoration, I received joy and can laugh again. After the cloudbursts and the violent raging storms passed over, I saw a bright rainbow of exquisite beauty splashed across the glorious blue skies. My cup overflows with Christ's blessings: *My cup runneth over. Surely goodness and mercy shall follow me all the days of my life: and I will dwell in the house of my Lord forever* (Psalm 23:5b, 6, KJV).

One of my favorite pastimes is to ride my bicycle on the pathway behind my house. It is a wildlife preservation area often frequented by deer, foxes, coyotes, and other critters. One day while riding I looked over in the meadow and saw a pair of white-tail deer grazing in the brush. Startled by some disturbance around them, they galloped gracefully away, looking as if their feet never touched the ground. I stopped to marvel at God's creation and realized that I, like the deer, am free to roam and to dance. My energy is renewed weekly as I participate in step-aerobics, weight training, and cardio-karate. In the summer when I mow the lawn, I do not complain anymore. As my legs stride purposefully down each long strip of freshly cut grass, I rejoice in my physical healing and thank God that I can walk. I even tried cross-country skiing and participated in the Bolder Boulder 10K race again.

I continued to wear my wedding ring for the first year following the accident. It was a gorgeous diamond solitaire, set in a contemporary gold band with delicate swirls. I experienced various mixed emotions as I looked at it each day. I was happy that Ken had given me this beautiful ring that symbolized our love and commitment to each other; yet, it saddened me to think that I was no longer married to this wonderful man. I took my wedding ring to a jeweler and had them remove the diamond and replace it with Ken's birthstone, a sapphire. The ring was resized to fit the middle finger on my left hand. I then selected a new gold setting for the diamond and wore it on my right hand. This step was so healing. Now I had two beautiful rings. The sapphire, reminded me of the joy that Ken and I had shared; the new setting with the diamond signified a beginning that was yet to come.

I stopped taking the antidepressants and now have control of my emotions again. I still have occasional bouts of depression, but my lows are not so low anymore. I still have chronic pain from my injuries, but it is tolerable now. And although I still long for a family of my own, God has given me contentment and peace in my singleness to seek Him first.

Both sets of scans that I underwent to test for signs of recurring cancer were negative. With extreme gratitude to my Healer, I have been free of cancer for more than four years. My doctors remain optimistic that the radioactive iodine treatment was successful and the cancer will remain in remission.

The Bolder Boulder again! Healed from the accident.
Me with friends Heather, Judy, Michele and Holly

I am truly blessed: *Blessed is he whose help is the God of Jacob, whose hope is in the Lord his God, the Maker of heaven and earth, the sea, and everything in them—the Lord, who remains faithful forever. He upholds the cause of the oppressed and gives food to the hungry. The Lord sets prisoners free, the Lord gives sight to the blind, the Lord lifts up those who are bowed down, the Lord loves the righteous. The Lord watches over the alien and sustains the fatherless and the widow (Psalm 146:5-9).*

I realized that the strength others passed off as mine was truly God's strength through Whom I am made strong, as Paul said: *That is why, for Christ's sake, I delight in weaknesses, in insults, in hardships, in persecutions, in difficulties. For when I am weak, then I am strong* (2 Corinthians 12:10).

God has given me His strength to share my testimony to churches, women's groups, youth events, and on radio and national television including, "Oprah," "The 700 Club," and Daystar's "Rocky Mountain Celebration," and "Living for Tomorrow."

Filming on The 700 Club

Sharing the gospel is like a two-edged sword. I speak to encourage the oppressed, yet they always seem to encourage me more. After I had spoken to a women's group, a partially deaf woman who had suffered physically through twenty surgeries, told me how much she liked the part of my story in which I used sign language to spell Ken's name. Her strength in overcoming adversity encouraged me greatly.

I do not know why some people are healed of incurable diseases while others suffer long painful deaths. Neither do I know why some people are safely snatched from the brink of impending danger while others suffer extreme brokenness in horrific accidents. Nevertheless, I do know that I serve a merciful sovereign God who lovingly said to me, "My beloved child, this is My will for you."

He never promised that I would not suffer, but He did promise to walk beside me and hold my hand. Through my brokenness, I have come to know God in ways that I never thought were possible. *The sacrifices of God are a broken spirit; a broken and contrite heart* (Psalm 51:17).

I have learned that with God nothing is impossible. Several years ago when I attended undergraduate classes and had to give speeches, my hands would literally shake and my heart felt as if it were pounding out of my chest. I have heard that the number one fear of all Americans is public speaking, and the number two fear is dying. Someone once jokingly said that people would rather die than do public speaking. I do not think that is true, but I do know that God conquered the fear of public speaking in my life. He gave me strength in that area because He wants to be glorified in my life.

I fulfilled my dream of attending graduate school when I earned a master's degree in curriculum and instruction from Colorado Christian University. God allowed this program to bring me to a place in my life where I could socialize and have fun again, although Ken's loss and the impact of the accident still weighed heavily on my heart. Returning to school was my first major step in beginning a new life and meeting challenges without Ken.

While I was attending CCU, my mother was attending Heritage Christian Center School of Ministry to become a missionary, and my dog was learning how to be a respectful canine in obedience school. Mom and I were thrilled both of us (and Cheyenne!) graduated with honors in the summer of 1997, and we decided to have a triple graduation party. Laughs were shared by all, since none of our family or friends had ever attended a graduation party for a dog before.

The course that influenced me the most in my master's program was a leadership class. It identified and redefined the active stance that we, as Christians, must take in leadership roles in our society. Jesus was the greatest transformational leader of all times.[1] He sought justice and truth, but was compassionate. He set guidelines and expected obedience, but was a servant to His disciples and washed their feet. His emotions were completely human, such as when He got angry with the sin in the temple and when He cried at Lazarus' tomb. He came to fulfill God's plan of redemption, and was obedient even unto death. I seek to be a leader who sets an example of Christ's love: to affirm, nurture, forgive and encourage.

The three graduates. Me, mom and Cheyenne.

I recently completed a four-week residency workshop in Virginia at Regent University, which began my exciting journey toward earning a doctoral degree in interpersonal communication. For the next four years, I will be studying via the Internet in their accredited distance education program. I will continue to write and speak with future aspirations of becoming a college professor.

One unfulfilled mission in my life was the taking of an active role in educating the public about railroad crossing dangers and trespassing laws. While searching the Internet, I came across a nationwide program for concerned individuals who do just that, called Operation Lifesaver, Inc. They instruct children, teens, and adults on railroad crossing safety. Working as a presenter for them, I will show a brief film presentation, share my personal experiences, and stress the importance of Operation Lifesaver's motto, "Always expect a train—look, listen, and live!"[2]

I have learned to live one day at a time and to trust in the sovereignty of God's plan. Sometimes when tempestuous storms linger above me, I grow afraid, then stumble and fall. Yet my heavenly Father reaches down with His strong arms, embraces me, and shelters me from the pounding rain. He is always there waiting with open arms to comfort me, hold me, and say, "Hold on, My beloved child, hold on!"

RAINBOWS AFTER THE RAIN

A cloud bursts, then the rain pours;
thunder roars like a lion.
Lightning bolt's metallic force
illuminates the gray sky.

My heart calms, as does the sea
when I rest in my Captain.
He guides my ship to dry land
and brings me to higher ground.

Once the storms of life are past,
I see the bright colored ray.
My destiny becomes clear.
Jesus Christ grants victory.

We passed the test, and now find
we can't contain His blessings.
With noble perseverance,
rainbows come after the rain.

Sherry M. Jones

God's Letter of Love

My faithful child, you have sown good seeds.
Wait but for a moment and My glory
will shine through as if it were a sun ray,
a bright powerful burst of My goodness.

I gave you a heavy cross to carry.
You mourned and questioned your losses, but
trusted Me with the faith I had given you.
I then healed your weary and broken heart.

I created you to carry out My plan.
Bring hope and sunshine to a hurting world.
My will—is for all to know Me as their Savior.
I do not wish for one child to perish.

My agape love is everlasting.
I gave you family and friends to love.
My greatest gift of love to you—My Son.
I love you more than you can imagine.

All things happen so I will be glorified.
I have numbered all the hairs on your head.
Your many tears have been stored in a vial.
I will direct you in the righteous path.

How sweet is the smell of the olive branch
that produces an oil of gladness.
I am your holy Oil of Gladness.
I will give to you joy unspeakable.

I am your mighty Rose of Sharon.
You are my dear tenderhearted flower.
Your gentle heart was breaking, but you
stood strong and endured the testing.

You gave Me the glory for your healing.
Our journey is long with many detours.
My child, remember that this is not
your final home; you are just passing through.

Always know I will never forsake you.
You are My child in whom I am well pleased.
When your life gets uncertain, call on Me.
I'll say, "Hold on My beloved child – hold on!

SHERRY M. JONES

Epilogue

He who testifies to these things says,
"Yes, I am coming soon."
Amen. Come, Lord Jesus
REVELATIONS 22:20

I pray that the experiences I have shared in my story encourage you to "hold on!" When it seems you have been forsaken, always remember that Jesus loves you and will never let you go! He is our Great Shepherd. Just like the shepherd in Luke, chapter fifteen, who left his flock of ninety-nine sheep to find the one little lost lamb that had gone astray, Jesus left His home to find you and me! I pray that you know Jesus Christ as your personal Savior. If you have not already done so, ask Him into your heart today. Your life will be changed forever!

Writing and poetic composition helped me to express my feelings without restraint. Reliving each painful experience during the three years that I wrote and edited my stories was difficult, and at times I felt like an artist who was recreating each scene of pain afresh on canvas. I questioned God's direction, but realized that if just one lost soul would come to know Jesus through my writings, then the pain I endured as I wrote each word was worth it.

After many laborious hours, vials of tears, and much healing, God gave me the strength to complete the task that He had assigned to me in the hospital. Sometimes we are asked to step out of our comfort zones, much like Noah was asked to do when he built the ark. He was not an ark builder, but he obeyed God's command. During one of my "being stuck" modes, God inspired the following poem:

Noah and I

Noah was obedient to God's commands,
one hundred plus years he built an ark on dry land.
People scoffed and said, "Hey, Noah, where's the rain?"
Yet Noah knew that God's love was foreordained.

Like Noah, I want to be obedient.
"Share your story with pen and ink," was God's intent.
Lord, I'm not an author, but You'll move my pen.
I'm stuck on this chapter, again and again.

People ask, "When will your book be revealed?"
God, show me to whom You'd have me appeal!
"I am glad you asked Me, My dear faithful one.
For this is why I sent My begotten Son:

Tell them I love them and will be there soon.
It may be in the morning, or night, or noon.
Don't worry about My arrival from above;
keep striving to tell My children of My love.

Life isn't fair or easy; for this, My Son died.
I do not wish to lose one soul who has cried.
I am the Solid Rock on which you can stand.
Like Noah, be compliant to My commands.

It's okay if you don't understand; meanwhile,
trust Me, for I want them all to reconcile.
I know the plans I have for you, My child.
In eternity, we'll meet in heaven's aisle."

Sherry M. Jones

I have often wondered, if years ago God had given me a tape to insert into in the VCR, entitled "Sherry Jones—This is Your Life," what I would have said? I imagine when it got to the beautiful wedding scene, and I saw my handsome prince, I would have smiled and said, "Oh, thank You, my gracious Lord! What a wonderful life I'm going to have!"

However, when we got to the cancer and the accident my gratitude would suddenly have disappeared, and perhaps I would have pleaded, "Oh, no, Lord, please don't let that happen!"

If I had known the character that God planned to create in me through my trials, I hope I would have said, "Okay, Lord, You know what You're doing. You're in complete control of my life."

Thankfully, God does not allow us to see our lives on videotape, but He does guide our steps and hold our hands along the way. As you travel down life's pathway, always remember that you are not alone. God will carry you through the harsh winter's storm into a victorious life of serving Him. Feel embraced in the arms of God throughout life's astounding journey.

DOWN LIFE'S PATHWAY

A childhood mem'ry I recall,
a dark and cloudy summer day.
Hail came thrusting from the sky up high
while I rode my bicycle's pathway.

I cried, "Please, Daddy, come rescue me!"
His strong arms sheltered me from the storm.
Heavenly Father, now protect me
from any turbulence that may form.

Jesus calmed the storm to a whisper.
"My child, I hear your weary plea."
I saw the palms of His loving hands
then knew He would never forsake me.

Sherry M. Jones

Then they cried out to the Lord in their trouble, and he brought them out of their distress. He stilled the storm to a whisper; the waves of the sea were hushed. They were glad when it grew calm, and he guided them to their desired haven (Psalm 107:28-30).

I will not forget you! See, I have engraved you on the palms of my hands (Isaiah 49:15b, 16a).

What Do I Say to the Brokenhearted?

And I will ask the Father,
and he will give you another Counselor to be with you forever—
I will not leave you as orphans; I will come to you.
JOHN 14: 16,18

*P*eople have often asked me, "What do you say or do for someone who has experienced tragedy or the death of a loved one?" Although there is not one specific answer to this question, I have outlined some of my personal experiences that I hope you will find helpful.

HELPFUL "DO'S AND DON'TS" FOR ENCOURAGERS TO THE BEREAVED

Do's

1) Listen.
2) Remember the deceased's birthday, anniversaries of his or her death, and holidays spent alone for at least the first few years.
3) Call frequently and encourage the bereaved—"I'm here for you."
4) Bring gifts of love, flowers, and food—anything to brighten their day.
5) Do favors for them (i.e., do house repairs, shovel the snow, make calls for them).
6) Create prayer chains (more prayer, more power).
7) Ask if they would like to share favorite memories of the deceased.
8) Offer personally to pray with them.
9) Allow them to freely express their tears and grief.
10) Send heartfelt letters and cards.

Don'ts

1) Don't give pat answers.
2) Don't be judgmental. ("Your family is cursed.")
3) Don't smile and act as if nothing has happened.
4) Don't offer insensitive advice. ("Go to church." "Snap out of it!" "Go volunteer.")
5) Don't say that your problems or someone else's problems are worse.
6) Don't ignore them because you feel helpless and don't know what to say.
7) Don't say "You're special," or "You're strong, because I couldn't go through that."
8) Don't try to point out how the tragedy might have been avoided. (Regardless—it happened).
9) Don't offer eloquent and poetic reasoning. ("God needed another angel in heaven," etc.)
10) Don't ask questions so that you can conclude the loss was justified.
11) Don't place expectations on them. (Baby showers, weddings, and parties are often difficult.)
12) Don't set a time limit on their grieving process. (It may take several years.)
13) Don't say, "I know how you feel." (Nobody truly knows how another person feels.)
14) Don't devalue their loss by saying that God will send something to replace it.

APPENDIX B

Happy Birthday, Dear Loved One

There is a time for everything,
and a season for every activity under heaven:
a time to be born and a time to die.
ECCLESIASTES 3:1, 2

Shortly before Ken's birthday the year following his death, my five-year-old niece Chanel said, "I miss Uncle Ken!" God used this precious child to comfort me, because I missed him, too. I had peace in knowing that Ken was experiencing eternity with our Lord, but on his birthday I still missed him even more than usual. After I prayed for God's comfort, He inspired the following invitation and poem. You may feel comforted to insert your deceased's name.

HEAVEN'S GALA EVENT OF ETERNITY

_____

Name

You are cordially invited to join
Heaven's Gala Event of Eternity
on

_____

Date of homecoming

Your reservation was made the day
you asked Me into your heart

I look forward to spending eternity with you,
My beloved child, in whom I am well pleased

Eternally Yours, Jesus

Happy Birthday, My Love

You received a personal invitation to join
Heaven's Gala Event of Eternity with our Lord.
I miss your loving presence, for on this day you were born.

I will forever hold your gift of love in my heart.
If I could blow out a candle and make one wish today,
I would tell you of my love that I have reserved for you.

Thank you for the joy you brought into my life.
Happy Birthday, my love, for now I celebrate alone,
but in heaven's great reunion we will both rejoice again.

Sherry M. Jones

End Notes

CHAPTER 2 - HELICOPTER TO HEAVEN

Photo credit: "Last family portrait" by Olan Mills.

CHAPTER 3 - GALLANT KNIGHT

Photo credits: "Special friends," "Uncle Harold," and "Me and my Knight" by All Pro Portrait Studios, Lakewood, CO.

CHAPTER 5 - THE ICU

Photo credit: "Crushed van," Courtesy of Iowa State Patrol.

CHAPTER 11 - OUR HOUSE

Photo credit: "Our first Christmas," by PCA International, Inc.

CHAPTER 13 - REALMS OF RADIATION

1. Qualmed Plans for Health (1999). *Underactive Thyroid* [On-line] http://www.qualmed.com/co/wellness/themes/july/theme4b.htm
2. Corrie ten Boom, *The Hiding Place*, (Old Tapen, NJ: Fleming R. Revell Company, 1971).

CHAPTER 14 - CELEBRATE KEN

1. "Never the Same" - Copyright 1995 by Oak Tree Music. All rights reserved. Used by permission.
2. Max Lucado, *Just in Case You Ever Wonder* (Dallas, TX: Word Publishing, 1992). Used by permission.
3. Sketch of Kenneth W. Jones, Jr. - 1995, by artist Joe Drnec.
4. 'Kin' with Jesus and the Angels - 1995, by artist Kami Henderson.

CHAPTER 15 - DEPRESSION

1. Steve Burns, MD & Kim Burns (1989). *The Medical Basis of Stress, Depression, Anxiety, Sleep Problems and Drug Use - Brain Chemical Messengers* [On-line]
http://www.teachhealth.com/chemmess.html
2. Mental Health Net & CMHC Systems (1995-99). *All About Depression & Depression Information* [On-line] http://depression.mentalhelp.net
3. Wil Pounds, Pastor South McGehee Baptist Church, McGehee, AR (1996-99) *The Causes of Depression* [On-line]
http://www.wilann.com/bpg/depcause.html
4. Obtained from the "Social Readjustment Rating Scale" by Thomas Holmes and Richard Rahe.
5. Statistics obtained from Operation Lifesaver, Inc. Visit their website at http://www.oli.org/oli

CHAPTER 16 - WALKING HAND IN HAND

(THE ACCIDENT SITE REVISITED)
Photo credit: "Three graduates," by PetsMart.

1. Leighton Ford, *Transforming Leadership -- Jesus' Way of Creating Vision, Shaping Values & Empowering Change,*
(Downers Grove, Il: InterVarsity Press, 1991).
2. Operation Lifesaver, Inc., is a nationwide, non-profit program dedicated to eliminating collisions, injuries and fatalities at highway-rail grade crossings and on railroad rights-of-way. If you wish to receive information on your state's Operation Lifesaver program, please contact: Operation Lifesaver, Inc. 1420 King Street, Suite 401, Alexandria, VA 22314 or call 1-800-537-6624.

COLOR INSERT PHOTO CREDITS:

Page 1: "Cheerleading" by Dean Studio, Golden, CO.
Pages 2 & 3: "Our wedding," and "Family at wedding,"
by All Pro Portrait Studios, Lakewood, CO.
Page 4: "Crushed van," and "Coupler of train," Courtesy of Iowa State Patrol.

For a small moment have I forsaken thee; but with great mercies will I gather thee. In a little wrath I hid my face from thee for a moment; but with everlasting kindness will I have mercy on thee, saith the Lord thy Redeemer (Isaiah 54: 7-8, KJV).

I have been…   BROKEN,

through life's trials,…   But

God has…   Not

                      FORSAKEN…me.

Order Form

Postal Orders:
Sherry M. Jones
P.O. Box 21
Parker, Colorado 80134

Please send me _____ copies of *Broken, But Not Forsaken*

@ $15.00 per book	_____
Colorado residents add $1.20 per book sales tax	_____
Shipping $3.00 for the first book; $2.00 for each additional book in USA, Canada, and Mexico	_____
Total Order	_____

Ship To:
Name:_____
Address: _____
City: _____ State: _____
Zip: _____

Telephone: (____) _____

Payment: Check _____

*International orders add $7.00 for the first book and $3.00
for each additional book. Quantity discounts available.*

Visit Sherry's Website at: http://members.aol.com/smjspeaks